Margareta Magnusson shared with the world the Swedish
tradition of döstädning – the practice of clearing out
unnecessary belongings – in her international bestseller
The Gentle Art of Swedish Death Cleaning.

Now, unburdened by baggage both real and emotional,
she reflects on her early days growing up in Sweden as
well as raising her family around the world, offering her
sharp wit and wisdom on how to age gracefully.

The Swedish Art of Ageing Well is a gentle and welcome
reminder that, no matter your age, there are always fresh
discoveries ahead and pleasures to be enjoyed every day.

The Swedish Art of Ageing Well

Also by Margareta Magnusson

Döstädning: The Gentle Art of Swedish Death Cleaning

The Swedish Art of Ageing Well

Life wisdom from someone who
will (probably) die before you

Margareta Magnusson

CANONGATE

First published in Great Britain in 2023 by Canongate Books Ltd,
14 High Street, Edinburgh EH1 1TE

canongate.co.uk

First published in the USA in 2022 by Scribner, an imprint of Simon & Schuster, Inc

1

British Library Cataloguing-in-Publication Data
A catalogue record for this book is available on
request from the British Library

ISBN 978 1 83885 949 7

Printed and bound in Great Britain by Clays Ltd, Elcograf S.p.A.

For my husband,
LARS

CONTENTS

SURROUND YOURSELF WITH THE YOUNG(ER) OR *BUSVISSLA* TO YOUR YOUNGER SELF

A lot of people past eighty complain about "today's youth." I don't. I like to have them around. They have new thoughts; they keep my brain fresh. They are a constant reminder that it is never too late to do anything, unless it really is too late (and you are dead). Until then, I still hope to tap-dance.

APPENDIX: BONUS THOUGHTS AND TIPS ON DEATH CLEANING

How to Broach One of Life's Most Important Topics with Your Loved Ones.

The World May Always Be Ending, but Spring Cleaning Always Arrives . . . Until the Day It Doesn't.

Death-Cleaning Discoveries in the Time of Covid and Answers to Other Questions I Have Received from Curious Novice Death Cleaners.

ACKNOWLEDGMENTS

PROLOGUE

The year I was born, the life expectancy for a Swedish woman was a little over sixty-six years and for a Swedish man was a little under sixty-four. My mother died at sixty-eight; she liked to follow the rules, while my father died at eighty-one—I'm sure he would have lived much longer if my mother had been there with him.

If I go by the actuarial tables, I should be long dead by now. If I go by the experience of most of my family, I'm practically a spring chicken at age eighty-six. My great-grandmother died at one hundred. Is it possible I could live for fourteen more years? It would seem so, but I think I won't. Or at least, some days, I hope I won't.

What does anyone do with one's time when one lives so long? Well, a few years back, one thing I did was write a book about a tradition we have here in Sweden. The tradition was sometimes called *döstädning*, literally in English "death cleaning," and because it is something that older women do—and society can often be very uninterested in older women's day-to-day lives—this practical, useful philosophy had not been noticed. So, I wrote a book called *The Gentle Art of Swedish Death Cleaning*; it came out in thirty-two countries and is aimed at all of us—even men!—who are in the latter half of life, though I have heard from a number of enterprising thirtysomethings who say they've already put the idea to work and have found it very useful, bringing calmness and order to their lives.

The idea is that we should not leave a mountain of crap behind for our loved ones to clean up when we die. Why would your family and friends want to take time out of their busy lives to clean up your mess when you clearly could have taken care of it yourself? Remember, your kids and your other loved ones may want some of your stuff when you are gone—not *all* of your stuff. So, we can help them narrow down the selection.

The book and the idea seemed to take on a life of their own once the book was published. For a year or two, I suddenly became very busy, much busier than I ever imagined I would be deep into my eighties. I found myself sitting for press interviews and answering questions about death cleaning from around the world, from Vietnam to the United Arab Emirates to Germany. I even traveled to London for the publication of the book there. In many of the interviews and articles, I was asked to show how I do my own death cleaning at home. By the time the whirl of press activity ended, I had death cleaned my little apartment so many times, I had practically nothing left!

I felt light and clearheaded. With all the stuff of my life no longer weighing on me, I began to refocus on what I would do now that I had no more death cleaning ahead.

If I end up following the footsteps of my great-grandmother, I might possibly have more than a decade of life still left to fill, so I began to look around me to see what remained, what I had in fact actually kept after all my death cleaning. I found I'd kept my memories and I now lived in a smaller, simpler way. I could actually see my life, now that there was less mental and physical clutter; I could enjoy my life more fully, even though of course there are other difficulties that come with ageing.

All my life I have been an artist and a painter. Suddenly I am a writer. I like it. But it is new.

The following essays are discoveries I have made about becoming very old—some of the discoveries were hard to accept, but many of them have been rather wondrous. In thinking and writing about them, my mind wandered to often pleasant and funny memories—and some not so pleasant or fun—that I hope will entertain you and take you to places and times you may never have experienced.

Much of this book was written while all of us were caught in the lockdowns and the pandemic—when death felt very near our doors and tragically claimed so many lives the world over. And yet in writing during that time, I was forced to focus on what made each day worth living.

I didn't want to write a long book. Old people don't want to read four hundred pages—they may not live that long. But I hope this book is also for younger people, who can get some tips about what to enjoy and watch out for as their own lives grow longer. Just like death cleaning, you can never start too early in preparing yourself for and understanding the ageing process, and the wonders and sorrows it will have in store for you.

In writing this book I have tried to include advice I myself needed as time marched forward, as history flapped by, as I stood in the middle of my own strange life and sometimes felt like a lonely pioneer, sometimes the happiest woman on earth, sometimes just completely clueless.

Is my advice particularly Swedish? Some of it. Are there secrets of Swedish ageing? Perhaps, and perhaps I have managed to unearth a few here. What I do know is that as a nationality we are certainly not as long-lived as the famous Okinawans of Japan, but Sweden is not doing too badly. Our current life expectancy averages 81.9 years, making us the thirteenth most long-lived country on the planet. If you are expecting that the Swedish secrets I will tell you will involve jumping into the frozen North Sea to stay young or taking long saunas, like some of my fellow older Swedes do, or eating ground-up reindeer horn in your morning muesli, I will disappoint you. I can't recommend these things, particularly if your constitution is not as strong as it used to be. Besides, I am sure I would not survive a frozen swim in the North Sea and would need to be very careful not to slip and fall in the sauna.

But perhaps my advice and discoveries are "Swedish" in that as a nationality, we tend to be quite blunt, clear-eyed, and unsentimental. Ageing is often difficult, but it doesn't have to be if you approach it in a way that isn't too filled with drama or with dread. And if you can find a way to make ageing itself into an art, where you are creative in how you approach each day, perhaps it can be a little easier.

Finally, because death cleaning really does not ever really end until you yourself do, I've included a little appendix to tell you about a few more tips I've discovered about perfecting your death cleaning, as well as answers to a few of the most often-asked questions that came up from readers.

So, yes, while I will always recommend continuing to death clean—your loved ones will thank you—remember that the process of death cleaning is ultimately in service to two larger points: to be less afraid of the idea of death, for it comes for all of us, and to remember that after you've death cleaned, no matter how ancient you become, there are always new discoveries, new mind-sets through which to see your life and the experiences you have had. And new and familiar pleasures to be had every day—even as the final visit of Mr. (or indeed Miss!) Death approaches.

MM

September 2021

HAVE A GIN AND TONIC
WITH A FRIEND

"Hello! Are you there? Hellooo! Can you hear me? . . . There you are! Hi! So good to see you again! . . . Yes, I've mixed my gin and tonic. Can't wait to try it. *Skål*, my little Lola! Mmm, so good, but maybe a bit chilly this close to Christmas. Maybe next week we try to warm up with some gluhwein instead. . . ."

Unfortunately, my best friend, Lola, doesn't live close by me in Sweden, but in France. It's a pity. On top of that, when we were in the middle of the pandemic it was hard, well, almost impossible, to meet up. I missed her.

But then again, now that technology has given us wonders like FaceTime, Skype, Zoom, Teams, WhatsApp, and other fun things, unexpected possibilities have opened up. It's important that we who are past eighty keep up-to-date with technology; otherwise we risk missing out on so much that makes modern life both easier and more enjoyable—not to mention we don't want our children and grandchildren to think that we're too old and square to participate.

All this new technology is also good for our friendships: now Lola and I can see and talk to each other as long as we want to on WhatsApp. And have a gin and tonic—or a gluhwein—together while we're chattering away. The warm and sweet gluhwein has kept people in the Alps alive for ages—it should work for us.

Lola and I have known each other for almost eighty years. When she was eight years old, her entire family moved to Gothenburg, a town on the west coast of Sweden where my family also made its home. Lola started in second grade at the same school as me.

I remember her being tall and thin, and that she almost always wore a dark blue dress with little white dots. I myself almost always wore a sensible skirt and sweater, which probably is why I remember her much cuter, prettier dress. Not because I wanted one too; it would not have suited me—but it was perfect for Lola. I was sure I wanted to be her friend.

We went on to spend our entire school life together, even though we chose different academic focuses—I explored art and design and Lola went to secretarial school. Lola had three great kids, and I had five. When I got married, I chose a man who would have to travel the world for his profession: we lived in the United States, Singapore, Hong Kong, and Sweden of course. No matter where we ended up on the planet, Lola and I always stayed in touch.

Later she became godmother to my second son, Jan (pronounced "yohn"), something the other four kids were deeply envious of. Somehow, Lola was more of a movie star than my other friends who got to be godmothers for the rest of the brood. Lola always wore the latest fashions, had a loud voice with a special international accent, loved to dance, had amazing hair, and looked great in a party hat.

During the summers when Lola and I were growing up, many who lived in the city moved out to cottages in the countryside, where they led easier lives and inhaled fresh air into their lungs. The cottages were often off by themselves, near enough to go to the little village to buy your food and basic provisions but not very close to other people. Being so far away from the crowded city was delightful, even though you of course occasionally longed for your friends.

Our family had a house some thirty to forty kilometers outside Gothenburg. As kids, we loved being there during weekends and holidays, and so did our aunts and other relatives who often came to visit. Friends visited too, including Lola.

In the spring we usually picked flowers, especially wood anemones. Lola was a star when it came to gathering them. No one understood how she did it. She would appear with beautiful, perfect handfuls of the pretty white-and-yellow flowers. Did she grab a fistful of flowers at once, and then another? No, she picked them one by one, quickly, and with great concentration. Then, because she was a good guest with a generous heart, she gave them to my mom, who put them in vases—one large bouquet from Lola and a smaller one from me.

We still laugh at all the things we got up to back then. Up in the attic, there was a big trunk tucked away. It wasn't left alone for long once we found it. The trunk contained very old clothes—long, tattered evening gowns that no one would want to wear today, hats decorated with flowers and veils, and one of those fox skins that ladies used to carry over their shoulders, complete with tail, paws, and a flattened head. What people won't do to be fashionable. But of course we played dress-up! It was such fun and how we laughed at ourselves for the way we looked. Then we clomped downstairs in our finery and went to greet neighbors and any guests who could bear us. Mostly only my mom could.

Lola and her family's summer home was on an island in the southern archipelago of Gothenburg. You got there by one of the white steamboats that departed from the "stone pier" in Gothenburg. Today it's the site of a fancy ferry terminal and the ferryboats are now much faster. You don't really have time to have lunch on board as we did back then.

Just traveling on the steamboat for a while felt like an exciting beginning to your stay. As soon as the boat left the harbor, I could feel that salty, wonderful wind that only exists on the west coast. I was a very independent little person, or maybe the times were different. I remember taking the tram to the ferry stop and getting on the boat by myself before I was even twelve years old.

Lola and her little brother met me at the tiny island jetty and then we took our time going to their home as we wandered through the island's small village. On the way they showed me the dance hall, the tennis court, and the house where another classmate, Erik, lived.

Some days we climbed the rocks to get to Erik's, to go swimming with him and his sister in the cold North Sea or sail in their dinghy. At times, we would crush a clam with a stone and fasten it to a string. We would lower the bait into the water and lie belly down on the dock for hours waiting for the little crabs to arrive and start to feed. Then we yanked them out of the water. After, we cooked them with dill and had a crab feast.

We would catch masses of crabs each summer. To this day still, I find them delicious.

Like me, Lola also moved around to many places in the world with her husband and kids, but we always tried to keep in touch. We managed to visit each other in Mölnlycke and Nice, Brussels, and Minneapolis. Even once in Dubai!

In those days, calling someone outside Sweden or in another country than where you were was something you didn't do unless it was very important. It was simply too expensive. Sure, we could have written letters, but in between infants and moving vans it was hard to find the time to sit down, or the peace of mind to collect my thoughts. Many times, so much had happened that I didn't know at what end to begin.

But Lola and I made the effort to get together. When

you've known somebody for so long, it's very easy to pick up where you left off, even if you have not seen each other. You know each other's backgrounds and families and how everything used to be. So, it is almost as if your conversation continues on like it was never interrupted at all—you talk again about events, both happy and tragic, travels, the children, schools, new acquaintances.

Wherever we lived we tried to come back to Sweden at least once a year. Coming back felt important to me. Not that I needed to feel like I was Swedish or belonged to the country but to meet up with family and friends and hear what they had been doing the past year.

Once in a while an elderly relative might have passed during my absence. It was sad and I tried to understand it was nature's way, even though I never fully got used to the shock of coming home to find they were not around anymore.

Now that I'm over eighty, it's becoming more common for people I know to suddenly not be around anymore. And it still doesn't feel natural at all. Most of us understand that nobody lives forever, but it's still a shock when the friend I recently spoke with is suddenly no longer available. Ever. The emptiness is at once so infinite.

Memory helps us retrieve events and people we want to remember. But my closest ones are always within and next to me—I don't need to think about things we did or said. Some people just become part of you. That feels comforting.

Anyhow, now it's gin and tonic time and I've been looking forward to this moment for a whole week. It's going to be so much fun. I can hear Lola's voice, hear the ice cubes clinking in her glass:

"Do you remember when we were twelve years old and—"

"We were Scouts and learned how to tie knots and dress wounds."

"And we went to camp with big backpacks, put up tents, and made big campfires. At night we'd sit around the fire and roast bread-on-a-stick."

"They were usually more burnt than tasty, but it was very cozy and we made a lot of good friends."

We toast, have a little sip, and laugh.

"Do you remember that time we traveled to Aix-les-Bains to do a language course?"

"Almost everyone fell in love—"

"We got to know a lot of boys, but not that much French."

And so on we went, picking up where we left off, recalling memories that only we remember. Soon our drinks are gone:

"Take care of yourself. . . ."

"We'll talk again soon. . . ."

Sometimes I wonder which one of us will be the first to not answer.

THE WORLD IS ALWAYS ENDING

Unusual times, uneasy days. I find it a bit reassuring that the paper drops through my mail slot at around four o'clock every morning. If it's a holiday, then there's no paper. I don't like holidays. Holidays used to be special days when stuff happened: family excursions, sporting events, sailing trips, swimming adventures, or even just mushroom picking in peace and quiet. Now, particularly in this pandemic era we are in, nothing happens on holidays. Not even the paper comes.

Sometimes, when it is not a holiday, I get up and peer out the window at this diligent person, going from door to door with the newspaper cart. Wondering if she feels it—that I am looking at her. Had it not been so early in the morning, I would have opened the window and shouted, "*Thank you!*"

The other day I read an article in my morning paper. A quote from actor Brad Pitt, who had played a meteorologist in a film, popped out like a knife. The article was about nature and weather, and his comment was in response to a question about what we might expect from the future. Pitt answered briefly:

"We have no future."

Unlike the North Pole these days, I froze when I read his remark. To an older person, the statement is true in many ways. Once you're past eighty, you generally don't have that much to look forward to anyway. We have to try to find something other than the future to be happy about. And once you begin to look, you realize the things to look forward to are all around you.

Like the present day, for example. I can be happy that my body feels all right today, that the sun might be shining, that a good friend agrees to go for a walk with me, and that we can enjoy all that is happening outdoors. Like when the ground becomes blue from blossoming *Scilla siberica* in early spring, the heat and greenness of summer, and come autumn the yellow leaves of the trees and the bloodred Virginia creeper trying to nestle its way onto my balcony. Oops, I'm thinking about the future now. How hard it can be to follow your own rules!

At my age you don't long for snow anymore, no matter how fun it once was to go sledding and skiing. Falling now isn't something you just jump up from, laugh about, and continue on. We mustn't and cannot fall. In the wintertime when I was a child, older people often got around in the snow by using a kick-sled. It is somewhat like a chair on a set of skies. One person sits on the chair; the other stands on the skis behind the chair and kicks the two of them along. I miss those rides. I think that for me these days kick-sledding might perhaps be ok, at least because I'd have something to hold on to.

But it still takes a lot of energy to move a kick-sled and I doubt I'd have the energy to drive a kick-sled today. I ask enough of my children already that I don't want to ask them to have to kick-sled their mother around Stockholm. Besides, kick-sleds are uncommon in the city these days. If I whizzed, or was whizzed, around in one, the people of Stockholm would no doubt laugh hysterically at me whizzing—or, more correctly, wheezing—by. Besides, I think I death cleaned my kick-sled long ago when I moved to the city from the country village where we lived before my dear Lars died.

• • •

Another thing I'm happy about is my old books. I like the books of Somerset Maugham—my husband introduced me to his work. I love Gabriel García Márquez, Tove Jansson, David Sedaris, Kristina Lugn, Kazuo Ishiguro, and many more. I don't want to get rid of any of them. Many new ones get published that I should perhaps read for a first time, but instead I read my old ones for the fifth, sixth, or seventh times. They are old friends.

The computer does bring me much joy, and also irritation, when it doesn't do what I had in mind. But perhaps I can get some help with it. Maybe from a grandchild or a neighbor, or an old techie friend! The computer certainly offers more than just a way to pay the bills. I can find out everything I've been wondering about on the computer: I can search for recipes, learn everything about the history of stripes—a pattern I love to wear—find out how a menstrual cup works, or get the backstory about a new pop song I heard on the radio. I can play solitaire. I can play games, write books, listen to all kinds of music, and watch TV shows that I've missed.

To meet friends of all ages over a coffee or a good meal can be so much fun. But in the time of corona it was unfortunately not that easy to arrange, especially in the winter. We had to put on our old winter clothes and meet on the balcony or in the park.

Thank God for the phone! My kids wonder why I insist on having two phones. They don't know my secret: I sometimes use the landline to call my cell to find out where on earth I've put it.

My second phone comes in particularly handy whenever I'm put on hold:

"We will handle your call shortly. Your place in line is three hundred and fifty-seven."

Then I can leave that phone on hold while I use the other one to do something more pleasant.

At my age I also think of all the bad things that can come with technological advances. Industrialization means pollution; plastics are great at the operating table but not in the ocean. Flying makes travel so easy—but at what cost?

It makes me sad that my generation and several before it treated the earth so poorly. But I hope Brad Pitt is not right. I hope we do have a future. Sometimes on very cold, dark, lonely winter days, I give in to his alarming pessimism too . . . until I remember that the end of the world has been at hand numerous times throughout history, as well as many times in my own lifetime. Yet, miraculously, the end still hasn't occurred, even though mine soon might.

Humankind has managed to survive other pandemics. My father, Nils, who was a doctor, taught me about the Spanish flu that ravaged the planet from March 1918 through June 1920. In Sweden alone, thirty-seven thousand people died from it.

Nils was young at the time, barely thirty years old. He told us of a family that lived close to his home where the mother and a teenage daughter had fallen ill. The disease ran its course very quickly; both were dead within a week. Everyone was worried, afraid even. My father told me that special hospitals were set up since the normal ones had become overcrowded, and that they were also working feverishly at the graveyards to care for all the dead. And even with all our technological and health care advances, a century later, the world didn't manage much better with the latest pandemic. Maybe the fear isn't that there is no future, but instead that humankind will just keep repeating itself, making many of the same mistakes.

It actually feels rather remarkable that I've lived for so long given that my lifetime has coincided with world wars, catastrophes, and cataclysms. Looking back, it's a wonder I didn't die of fright. Maybe I just didn't understand the seriousness of the situations that arose. Or maybe it is that no one has the strength to be terrified for more than short periods of time. Humankind somehow continues to stagger along, surviving even the darkest times.

When World War II broke out in 1939, I was too young to understand how horrible this was. But I did notice how worried and tense my parents were. Television hadn't arrived yet, but they listened to the radio a lot. Since the radio reception was sometimes bad, we children had to remain calm and not make too much noise. It crackled and sputtered, but every now and then we could hear a man screaming—one of Hitler's speeches being broadcast. He frightened us.

During one particularly turbulent period, my sister and I were evacuated for a couple of months from Gothenburg. Gothenburg is one of Sweden's great port towns and therefore was considered a prime target. So Mom drove me and my sister inland to stay with one of her best friends, who could take us in at their family farm. It wasn't especially fun to have to leave everything at home and wave good-bye to Mom, but our evacuation to the countryside turned out to be nicer than we could have imagined.

The farm was big and well managed. The family lived off the land, selling all the produce that the animals and crops supplied them with, but all this produce required labor.

Farm work begins very early each day, but I, who had not yet turned ten, was allowed to get my sleep and wake up on my own. Breakfast was left out on the table until ten in the morning, so I was alone to pick my fill from the bread, butter, marmalade, and eggs. There was a happy-looking stuffed cloth hen on the table. If I put my hand up the buxom hen's butt, I could immediately feel the boiled eggs, still warm. Yummy!

There were many animals on the farm—cows and calves, horses, some pigs, chickens, and turkeys. It was my job to feed the turkeys. A position of great trust, I felt. They ate a goo of oats and chopped hard-boiled eggs and other things I've forgotten. The turkeys made a gurgling sound as they came hopping toward me, realizing it was dinnertime. I was afraid of them and rushed to give them their water and food. I always felt relieved when I closed the door to their enclosure behind me.

I felt more at home accompanying Mom's friend as she worked to grow white asparagus. I watched, fascinated as she would cup the sandy earth around each of the plants and how she harvested the asparagus in early summer.

Mom's friend was kind and also funny. Sometimes, after dinner, she would tell stories about the other people from the countryside. I especially remember this one: A pastor was traveling on the road when he met another carriage. The road was a bit narrow, so the pastor's driver called out to the old man traveling in the opposite direction:

"Move, you old coot; can't you see it's the pastor who's coming?"

"Why, yes," the old man said leisurely, "but the road won't get no wider because of that."

Her stories were always filled with all sorts of local people, who usually had a lot more common sense than the grand "so-and-sos" who also often showed up in the stories.

Sometimes, when the farm's workhorse wasn't working, I was allowed to ride the giant Clydesdale bareback. Even though I had not ridden horses much, he seemed to understand everything I said to him. He went where I wanted him to go. When we got back to the farmhouse and I wanted to get off, he halted gently.

And yet, far away out somewhere else in the world, the bombs fell and gas flooded the chambers.

I couldn't know it at the time, but when I think back to it now it seems unbelievable that the extreme horrors and the simple joys of the world can exist simultaneously.

But I wasn't completely oblivious to what was going on. When we got back to Gothenburg, we couldn't help but learn more, as we heard our dad and mom discussing that day's events over the dinner table. For months it seemed as if the world might end any day.

I will never forget May 7 when we understood there would again be peace. Everyone went crazy with relief and joy. There was great commotion on the street outside our house. Of course I wanted to go out to look and take part. To my great surprise that day, nobody stopped me.

Out on the main street, Kungsportsavenyn, there were tons of people singing and shouting and making noise. From the windows they were waving flags, scarves, and handkerchiefs. Some people even emptied their trash bins out the windows so that the air was full of whirling pieces of paper. Had I wanted to go home, it would have been difficult because the streets were so crowded. There wasn't much else I could do, so I followed along with the people. Everybody was pushing toward the main square, Götaplatsen, which was the heart of the city and where there would be speeches and singing.

I had never seen so many people gathered around the

statue of Poseidon in the city center. I biked around that statue with my friends sometimes in the evenings. The place was usually empty, but this evening we were more like packed sardines. At one point, I lifted my feet from the ground to see what would happen. I didn't fall down! It felt a bit uncomfortable to be so wedged in, but the crowd soon dissolved. I ran home and recounted everything I had experienced.

More than thirty years later, I went through the same experience in Tokyo's subway: if you lift your feet from the floor during rush hour, you don't fall down either. The unfortunate Japanese commuters around me did not appreciate my experiments.

At school, the peace sparked a lot of conversation. The teachers were kind enough to let us share our thoughts, one at a time so that everyone could hear what was on each speaker's mind.

I attended a secular school. Unlike other schools, everyone was welcome, and no kid had to wait on a bench outside the classroom because Christianity was on the curriculum. Instead we had a subject called Religious Studies and were taught just as much about Vishnu and Buddha as Jesus and the Holy Spirit.

From my neighborhood friends I learned that other schools had religious gatherings every morning, where they sang Psalms that they were then assigned to learn by heart.

At my school, it was different. We had gatherings on Saturdays. One of the teachers—or an invited guest—would tell a story from a journey they had taken or some other interesting thing they had seen. Occasionally, someone played the piano or showed slides. I still don't know any Psalms by heart.

Because of its religious tolerance, many parents who belonged to different faiths sent their children to this school. Several of my best friends were Jewish and we spent our days together. During the war, but also for a number of years after, I got notes in my mailbox warning me that I should choose my friends more carefully, telling me not to spend time with a specific few of them. Of course it made me very sad, upset, and angry, but I disregarded the anti-Semitic messages and continued to be friends with the people I chose.

In the 1970s, my husband and I lived in Maryland and in the '80s in Singapore. In Singapore, besides the local school, there was also a French, an English, and an American school. Since our children went to an American school while we were living in the States, the most reasonable thing was to continue on in that education system, even though we were living almost ten thousand miles away from America.

Soon our family was absorbed by school life. The kids participated in a bunch of American pastimes, activities such as synchronized swimming, football, and cheerleading.

My husband and I often spent entire Saturdays up in the stands, watching our sons play ball games and daughters cheer them on. Those days were long. The heat was tropical and the men in the commentator booth drank beers to cool off. All day. When the last game started around 9:00 p.m., they were usually quite tipsy. They mispronounced the names of the players, made crude but funny jokes, and commented on people they recognized in the audience:

"Look, folks, that's Terry Barns—recently discharged after painful hemorrhoid surgery. Give him a hand!"

Sometimes we were invited to accompany friends on their boat. To someone who had grown up on the coast, it was such a delight to get out on the water. We swam right off the boat, while our hostess prepared a tasty and salty curry stew with crabs and fish heads. The dish was served on leaves from a banana palm tree next to mounds of rice.

One weekend, another friend's family needed a deckhand. They were sailing their boat from Jakarta, the capital of Indonesia, on the island Java, to Singapore. Since the boat owners knew we were a family of sailors, they asked if we could help. My youngest son, Tomas, then age seventeen, was intrigued and expressed his interest. To sail on the South China Sea, among spice islands, sharks, giant jellyfish, and corals, sounded exciting. The trip would take three days.

Tomas's adventure became more of an adventure than any of us could have imagined.

The skipper had made the trip to Singapore from Java so many times that he felt completely sure of the course to take and had been sloppy about bringing all the necessary sea charts along for the trip. Two hours out of Jakarta the battery of the engine died. Unfazed, they set sail for a few hours, until suddenly the running backstay—an important part of the rigging—broke.

The skipper tried to reach out to other ships in the area, but to no avail. Because he'd forgotten the charts, the skipper realized too late that the boat had drifted into a coral atoll so narrow that it was impossible to turn around.

An anchor tied to a long rope was loaded onto a life preserver and my son Tomas swam out as far as the rope stretched and dropped the anchor down. Once it caught on the seabed, the people on the boat used a winch to pull the boat, stern first, as close to the anchor as possible. Then the anchor was pulled up, placed on the life preserver once more, and Tomas was sent to swim out again. By this process, the boat was laboriously inched backward out of the coral narrows—the procedure had to be repeated countless times until the boat was freed and could be steered bow first.

At home in Singapore, three days had passed; we had not heard a word and were becoming more and more alarmed. One of my daughters, who was deeply Christian at the time—she was ten—had the whole church praying for her big brother. She was so sad and anxious. I myself walked around with a big knot in my stomach; I couldn't think of anything but my son and at night I couldn't sleep. We could make no contact through the VHF radio. I thought the world would end.

The coast guard was alerted, since it wasn't uncommon for sailors to be attacked by pirates in the South China Sea. But the coast guard only patrolled Singaporean waters and it was very possible the boat was somewhere outside their jurisdiction. I hardly dared to imagine what else might have happened.

After another day with no word, and out of pure despair and mad with worry, my husband, Lars, rented a small plane and hired a pilot. They flew out over the islands and the sea to look for our missing son. All that blue and green must have shimmered below, but of course no one could enjoy its beauty. All my husband wanted was to find his son.

Finally, Lars spotted the boat from the air. Very slowly, it was drifting in the right direction toward Singapore, but the wind was still nonexistent, the sails flapping. Somewhat relieved, Lars and the pilot returned home and called the coast guard to give them the boat's rough location. Thankfully the boat had managed to make it into the Singaporean coast guard's realm and the coast guard was able to find them and lead them home.

The following day we welcomed the missing sailors to Singapore. The trip had taken seven days instead of the estimated three. Tomas was in good spirits; it had been the adventure of a lifetime. The world had not ended. Not for me and certainly not for him.

My husband, Lars, was incorrigible, but maybe he should have learned something from the trauma with Tomas.

Lars loved the sea, its creatures, and any sort of boat, so he would grab any opportunity to be on one.

One Christmas a year or two later, we decided to go sailing with our family along the western coast of Malaysia toward the Strait of Malacca. We had met a couple who owned a big catamaran that they invited paying customers on board for multiday sails around the South China Sea. The husband was English and served as the skipper; the wife was Thai and did the cooking. We missed our lovely family cruises around Bohuslän, on the west coast of Sweden, and decided to charter the catamaran instead of trying to make the complicated and expensive trip home to Sweden that December. At least if we stayed in Singapore for Christmas, it would be warm enough to sail.

Perhaps we should have thought it over a bit more.

We were really looking forward to spending Christmas week on board. We were lucky—the sun was shining and there was just the right amount of wind. The day before Christmas Eve we made a foray ashore onto one of the many empty islands that are dotted throughout the South China Sea. It felt nice to walk barefoot on the white, soft sand, as opposed to the hard flooring of the boat.

On the beach we found a sturdy branch and decided to make it our Christmas tree; we brought the branch aboard and dressed it with shells and corals. As we got back out to sea again, we soon noticed an approaching boat. From a distance it looked worn down, almost as if it was homemade. Smoke spewed out from its engine area. For a long while the boat followed us at a distance; then it started to creep closer and closer. It was scary.

Our skipper became more and more concerned. He reluctantly let us know that our followers might well be pirates; in the Strait of Malacca they are not the people you want to meet. Modern pirates of the South China Sea are like pirates of earlier eras: when they reach your boat, they board, cut your throat, and rob you of anything valuable.

The worried skipper fetched an object that from a distance could be mistaken for a gun. He kept it pointed toward the approaching boat. The passing minutes felt like an eternity as the boat got closer. Then suddenly the boat changed course and disappeared far out to sea, spewing smoke behind it as it went.

That day, the world did not end either.

Looking back, I realize I rarely worried for my children. Maybe I should have more. No matter where we were in the world, people have generally been kind and helpful, despite us being foreigners. And my kids have been wise, most of the time, and in their teens they generally managed to stay out of harm's way.

Singapore may sound a bit dangerous, but my kids never got into trouble. At night, I let them stay out as long as they wanted to, but they always came home at a sensible time. Their American friends, on the other hand, were always being watched and had strict rules and curfews to follow, with severe punishment if they didn't comply. Perhaps unsurprisingly, it was these tightly controlled kids who often got into the most trouble.

I have had so many worries—but the world is still here. So are my kids.

. . .

I often reminisce about that day when the war was over, the euphoria we all felt. But the joy didn't last long. The growing conflicts between the West and the East did not result in an ordinary war, but they still left decades of uneasiness hanging over us.

Nuclear war began to feel like a constant threat, something I often had to talk to my kids about. And soon more catastrophes and calamities: Chernobyl, just several hundred kilometers away, its radiation reaching Sweden's shores. Or AIDS. Or the fact that everything is carcinogenic. The world is always ending, and yet it continues to survive.

We must always hope for a sustainable future, but hope alone is not enough. Even if we ourselves may not live to see it, we mustn't be so preoccupied with living in the present that we forget to leave room for—and help prepare for—a possible future. The philosopher Kant said that at every turn and action you must ask yourself: "What if everyone did this?"—it is a good rule. It helps me figure out what is right and wrong. Imagine if we all did this? Even at my age it is not too late to start.

Then the world will never end.

DON'T LEAVE EMPTY-HANDED

A very clever woman I know—or knew, as she passed away some time ago—had a natural tidiness about her. Her name was Birgitta and she was the owner of the Gothenburg art gallery where I had my first exhibition in the late 1970s.

Birgitta's art space was a storefront with a short stairway, five steps down from the street level. People were always dropping in and out to look at her artists' works. Her space was on the main street for art galleries in Gothenburg. That street was also the main street for streetwalkers: I remember a blond woman who would come in wearing high heels, look at the art, and then walk back out again. During the day she sometimes turned up as a brunette in slippers. I didn't mind: art lovers come in all shapes and sizes. We are all a big family. She would point at a work of art and say:

"That I like."

It happened sometimes that the work she liked was mine. I was so proud. She was my favorite customer.

To the left of the entrance to Birgitta's art space there was a big table made of light brown marble looking like toasted meringue, a table around which the cultural celebrities of Gothenburg (there were not many; Gothenburg is not a big city) would gather to have coffee, drink sherry, talk art, and argue politics all through the day and night. I did not participate in the nighttime sessions—I was a square with five children—but I do know that Birgitta had a slogan she would softly shout at anyone who stood up to go to the bathroom, or to go to her little kitchen to get a snack or more sherry:

"Don't leave empty-handed [*Gå inte tomhänt*]!"

Birgitta was not instructing her guests to pluck pieces of art from the walls and take them home. She simply wanted everyone to help clean the table bit by bit as the day turned into night. Since they were going inside anyway, they could help by taking something with them. Her gentle order was simple, friendly logic. She said it to everyone, from the CEO of Volvo to the head of the Gothenburg art museum, from her interns to her artists. All were asked. Nobody protested. Everyone helped.

I saw how her slogan was very effective and so I started practicing her technique with my children at home. In no time at all it was part of our daily routine—and it wasn't just for clearing the dinner table.

I think the principle of not leaving empty-handed can be applied everywhere you go in life. If there are dirty clothes on your bedroom floor and you pass the laundry basket empty-handed, that is not clever. The pile will only get bigger. Don't leave empty-handed.

When heading out the front door, take the garbage with you. Don't leave empty-handed. When entering your house, don't step over the mail on your welcome mat—pick it up! Don't leave empty-handed.

A friend called Maria has another approach to making sure she is not overwhelmed by her things. Her rule is that if she brings anything new into her house, she must take something that she already owned out of her house—to be given away, donated, sold, or recycled. She is hard-core. At first it was just books. If she bought a book, she had to get rid of one. She felt this worked, so she applied the same to clothing, shoes, makeup, body lotion, scarves, shampoo, aspirin. Yes, even food.

These days her cupboards are tidy, as are her closets, bookshelves, and bathroom. There are no stacks of things that need to be sorted or shelved. Nothing just sits around and collects dust. Sometimes she even gets rid of things without having acquired anything new. That is where we all need to be.

The more I've thought about it, the more I realize that Birgitta's simple saying could apply to almost any situation in life. Sure, as I've said before, when you leave earth make sure there is not a bunch of your crap still here for someone else to deal with after you go.

But also, while you are still on earth, make sure the planet itself has been a little bit picked up after before you go. Difficult—yes. I am not asking you to take responsibility for everything since Ford invented the assembly line—but look around at the world you live in. What can you do?

Soon after *The Gentle Art of Swedish Death Cleaning* was published, one of my children sent me an article about a lawyer and activist named Afroz Shah, who devoted his weekends to picking up rubbish along a polluted beach in Mumbai. His dedication had inspired others and now each weekend thousands of volunteers, even celebrities and politicians, show up to clean the beach. They had picked up thousands of tons of trash. The article in *The Week* quoted him as saying, "Don't make it an event. When we clean our houses every day, do we make it an event? It's a daily affair whether we like it or not. Cleaning and protecting the environment must also be like this."

One of my children and I joked that Mr. Shah "*döstädade planeten*"—he was death cleaning the planet. And then we talked about his work seriously—everyone should be death cleaning the planet. It should be mandatory, a couple of hours a week. Almost like a military service. The planet isn't cleaning itself.

A lot of people go shopping on weekends, buying stuff wrapped in plastic that often ends up in the ocean. Mr. Shah cleans up instead. So can you. It may be the little park near your apartment building, or the beach where you swim, or the highway you drive to work. I love the American author David Sedaris, who lives in Sussex, England. Instead of just power walking to stay fit, he cleans the roadside while he walks. He has a trash picker and a garbage bag that he carries with him; he is so effective that he recently had the honor of having a garbage truck named after him.

I pick up cigarette butts from the streets around where I live. I used to be a heavy smoker and I feel a bit guilty about that, but with my walker stroller and wielding my trash picker I feel the absolution like a strong nicotine rush.

There is a young Dutch man named Boyan Slat who has devised a plan to clean up the Pacific Ocean. He is amazing; he is taking responsibility for plastic I probably threw into the water when we were out dodging pirates in the South China Sea back in the 1980s. Yes, I remember the captain taking a full bag of trash, punching holes in it with an ice pick, and heaving it into the ocean, where it sank beneath the waves. We were quite horrified. Even back then in Sweden we never threw trash into the water or left garbage in the woods; but as guests on his boat and relying on him to protect us from pirates we dared not argue. Thank goodness that Boyan Slat has started a movement at sea to clean things up.

The truth is my generation has been really horrible when it comes to pollution and has been very hard on the planet. Now very late I realize I must help clean up. Most of us are too old to head to India to clean up the beaches or pick up crap on the highway, but we are not too old to get involved. We can organize; we can influence; some of us can donate, if not money, at least time. So, I support Greta Thunberg and all the young people who are trying to save the planet. I support old people who try as well.

I would like to leave the planet with the woods looking like they did when I was a girl. I would like to see Bali surrounded by healthy coral reefs as it was when I was there in 1979. Today people on the beach collect bottle caps instead of shells—but at least cleaning up bottle caps is more constructive. A friend of mine had a daughter who visited the Gili Islands outside Lombok in Indonesia. There were a lot of beggars on the beach and few tourists gave them money. So my friend's daughter organized the beggars into groups to pick up the garbage on the beach and asked for donations to help support the cleanup mission. Presto: the sunbathers opened their wallets right away.

When I am gone I want to have helped clean up the world. I understood much too late in life that this is important. But I am not dead yet and will spend every spare minute I have to live up to Birgitta's motto.

Don't leave empty-handed—not this planet, not even your life.

Clean up after yourself as you go along.

I DIED SEVEN YEARS AGO—
BUT LIVED

Most people are scared to die.

I died seven years ago and it happened so fast that I didn't even have time to be afraid.

It was early February and the Gothenburg Film Festival was going on. I traveled down from Stockholm and was so happy about it. I was going to meet up with some of my children and a few other nice people and we were all going to go to the premiere of a film made by one of my children. Afterward, I would spend the night at a friend's house.

The weather was slushy, as it often is in Gothenburg. Big, wet snowflakes turned into puddles as soon as they hit the ground.

My friend and I took a taxi from the movie premiere and went home to watch television and talk some, but as soon as we got in the door I immediately sensed that something was very wrong. It was as if all my strength had disappeared. I told my friend I felt a little off and would go to bed early. I managed to undress, slip into my nightgown, and get to bed. Then I wasn't there anymore. It happened that fast! My friend only knew because she passed my room and saw that I had not folded my clothes as neatly as I usually do.

My wise friend called an ambulance. With the help of my cell phone, she located some of my children. I have no idea how we got down in the small elevator with its ancient gate. I don't remember any of it, but very quickly we were on our way to nearby Sahlgrenska University Hospital, where they admitted me right away. I was unconscious the whole time and didn't know or feel anything. Those hours are like a parenthesis in the midst of my life.

All of this probably took an hour. When I woke up, I found myself in a very bright, yet small, room with a smiling young woman beside me who was soon joined by a similarly smiling young man, both intensive care nurses.

They said hello and joyously welcomed me back to the world. It all seemed so improbable, but their joy was infectious. Soon we were talking and laughing together. If these young people hadn't worked so hard at bringing me back to life, I would still have been unconscious and eventually dead. And I wouldn't even have noticed. It had all happened so fast.

Slowly, slowly, it dawned on me that I had just gotten my life back.

"Did you see any angels?" "Did you see any light at the end of the tunnel?"

These are questions I've been asked many times since. My answer was "No," which seems to disappoint some of my questioners. I really hadn't expected my answer to be "No" either—if I ever survived death, I don't know what I expected, but what I got was: nothing!

The truth was simply that it was as if someone had flipped the on-off switch. I know that many people believe they will meet their friends and loved ones once they are dead. I don't, although I can see how that would be a comforting, positive thought. Maybe I'm not a big believer in seeing life from only the positive, from only one side. Perhaps also I am a bit too Swedish and practical minded; when I think of an "over there" where we are going to meet our friends and loved ones again, wouldn't we also have to meet all our enemies there too? No thanks. Not for me. I think that when it's over, it's over.

By contrast, as I sat in that bright little room with those two young people's bright, warm faces, I felt very happy. I existed. Again.

Within an hour or two, my two beaming companions brought me up to a regular, open ward. Since it was the middle of the night, we kept quiet as two other patients were already lying there asleep in the dimly lit space.

Once they had settled me, another young female nurse came and sat by my bed. I suppose she was meant to keep me awake a bit. She managed to pass the time by telling me all about her life. It wasn't tedious, just pleasant, and she had lots to tell. She was a single mom to two small boys, four and five years old, living in the small town of Alingsås, about a half hour outside Gothenburg. Soon she was going to catch the train home. Once she was home, she and her sons were going to play with LEGOs; it was Sunday after all. I didn't need any riveting stories, just listening to her talk about her everyday life was comforting and very soothing.

As morning arrived, the doctors made their rounds and

suddenly a small circle of friendly surgeons surrounded my bed. I was told a valve in my heart had burst and needed to be stitched together as soon as possible. It felt as if they had already sharpened the knives and polished the needle, so eager were they to get me into the surgical theater.

When I think about the operation I had that day it feels like I was outside myself, looking down on everything like it was a film shot from above, only perceiving the sound of running feet, doors opening and closing, and people I didn't know bending over me. I was on a rolling sea without any steady footing, with lots of nasty, tiny, brightly colored creatures hovering around me.

Eventually, the strange, muffled chaos passed and as I returned to normalcy I found my children waiting for me, surrounding me. Of course, I was so happy to see them and a few friends who had been nice enough to come by. But what havoc I had caused! Sometimes it is a bother to get old, but they all had patience with me and I was very grateful.

My experience is that when you lose a beloved friend there really is no "proper" way of dealing with it. When a person suddenly dies of, say, a heart attack or in a traffic accident, it is a terrible shock to any close relatives and loved ones. If, on the other hand, the person has been ill for a long time and has been cared for at home, it can instead feel like a relief, even if you do not want to feel that way at all. Putting your friend's needs in the front seat and your own in the back is not good for anyone in the long run, especially if their illness goes on for a long time.

The ones left mourning suffer too. As a mourner, no matter how many times you have been one before, you are never familiar with this new situation, a life without the friend who just departed. It is not until after a funeral and everything else that follows—the rituals and bureaucracies after a death—that a completely different life can begin to take shape.

My life became so empty and desolate after my husband died. He was my very best friend. We had been through so much during our almost fifty years as a couple and we had cried and laughed so many times together. We had shared each other's experiences and given each other encouragement. I know how my husband would have thought about many difficult issues, how he would have acted in various situations. I still think: What would Lars have done now? I miss him terribly, but I feel him with me all the time. I even ask him for advice now and then. I carry our life together inside me. Our thoughts, our fun, our troubles, are all treasures that no one can ever take from me.

I was born in Gothenburg. I died there once. But since Gothenburg wasn't my place of residence, I had to be transferred by plane to Stockholm, where I was registered. While the benefits of Sweden's national health care system are many, in order for it to run smoothly they do have a lot of processes and systems by which we all must abide.

A female nurse, a pilot, and me on my rolling gurney took off in a small plane. I had my head against a tiny window and could see everything that was happening outside, even though the weather was foggy and not especially good. The nurse told me that they had already made one patient transport earlier that day and that after they had dropped me off, there was another waiting to be collected in the north of Sweden. No rest for them!

The rain was pouring down when we landed. The drops felt good on my face, but then someone stuck an umbrella over me. Christ, how crappy it is not to be able to decide anything for yourself, or do anything on your own. Only having to be grateful for the care your caregivers give all the time. Which I really was, no question.

Swedish health care is amazing; all this was almost free, though of course in truth I had paid my taxes toward it for a very long time. So, I decided not to feel guilty, though I did wish I had felt more of that soothing rain on my parched face.

At Karolinska University Hospital outside Stockholm, I asked for a small radio that I listened to under the covers so as not to disturb anyone when I could not sleep. On the hour, every hour, I heard the chime for the news. I listened intently for that chime to make sure I was really alive: each time it sounded I knew that I was.

Almost as quickly as my downward spiral happened, everything progressed back to normal. I was home again, without even having to think about it. I was summoned daily for physiotherapy: a date had been made for a check-in with the doctors. All my appointments and instructions were waiting for me in the mailbox when I got home. All I had to do was get out my diary and mark down the dates.

Well, not really! I was moving more slowly and was much less mobile, so just getting to the building where the physiotherapy took place seemed to take all morning, and getting back seemed to take all afternoon.

Once I got to the building, the hallways seemed to go on for miles, while picking the right elevator was a feat. I found it so tiring that some days I wished I had never woken up in that intensive care unit.

The physiotherapy, once I got there, was so great it was worth all the hassle. I could feel myself getting stronger after every visit, not something you are used to at my age, when every day is usually about getting weaker. I almost felt young again, or at least at some younger age where each day meant health. I truly missed going there when it was over. I learned something I had never really known before: when you are in rehab after heart surgery there is no point in trying to feel comfortable and there is absolutely no point in complaining. You just have to do the work—however painful it might be.

When you are my age, you will probably meet people who are scared to die. I have been to the hospital so many times and visited friends and family who no longer can get out of bed or care for themselves that I think we should not be scared of death but of living too long. When death comes, just hope it is quick. Take it from me, someone who lived through death, it does not have to be unpleasant at all.

VOLUNTEER AS MUCH
AS YOU CAN

After my husband passed away, I cleaned out our house and moved from a small fishing village on an island on Sweden's west coast to a two-room apartment in our capital city of Stockholm.

I had few friends in the area, and having retired I didn't have much to do during the day. I kept myself busy every way I could think of. I bought a leather jacket that I thought looked good. I joined social media; I started a blog about art. After many years on an island I was in a deep need for culture, so when I hit Stockholm I went to art galleries all the time, attended concerts, hosted lunches, and tried to help people my age who were not as mobile as I. Above all, I volunteered to take care of the garden in the co-op I had moved into. I love gardening and have learned that it really doesn't matter whose garden it is—as long as I have access and can see stuff grow, I am happy. And volunteering is great fun too.

Volunteering makes you feel useful and good about yourself; it was something I learned quite by surprise when I was forty and our family moved to the United States.

• • •

In our home we always ate dinner quite late. Even when the kids were little and we were still living in Sweden. We probably ate far too late for what is considered correct for children. But we kept our evening dining a secret. The children got a free hot meal in school every day, so we knew they wouldn't starve, and we believed it was important and nice that we met together each day, Dad included. The dinner table was the perfect spot, even if it might be at 8:00 p.m., God forbid.

With five children, two adults, and often a pet or two, our dinners were usually quite lively. There was a lot of talking. We had all been through a whole day's worth of experiences since we had seen one another last, and everyone wanted to share the highlights of their day.

I especially remember one autumn dinner; it must have been a Thursday since we had just finished the Norwegian seafood soup that we ate every Thursday and were about to dig into the pancakes, which the children liked quite a bit more.

In Sweden, soup (often split-pea soup with bits of pork) and pancakes is on every menu and table on Thursdays. It's a relief not to have to think about what to cook. But a bit strange too—an entire country eating the exact same thing. Also, yellow pea soup, although delicious, makes everyone farty. I wonder how much methane Sweden releases every Thursday.

I cannot remember any time I asked my children to be silent when we had dinner. The intention was that we should all talk. This particular Thursday my husband, Lars, took his spoon and clinked it against his glass, as if he were going to give a speech.

I knew what he was going to say, but the kids gaped in anticipation. Clearly, they all felt sure that something important was about to be said. It became very quiet in the room. After what felt like an eternity Lars spoke:

"This spring we will move to America."

All kinds of looks were exchanged: happiness, fear, surprise, confusion. Again it became absolutely quiet around the table as everyone considered this news. Finally, someone asked:

"Where is that?"

And then the floodgates opened as everyone thought about their own special situation and how the move would impact them. Johan, the oldest, was in high school. Jane, the youngest, was about to start first grade.

There were so many questions that needed answers:

"What is the food like?"

"Can we bring the dogs?"

"Will we see Indians? Cowboys?"

"Do they speak Swedish?"

"Do they have Scouts?"

"Do we have to go to school?"

"Will we get to drink soft drinks every day?"

"What kind of animals do they have there?"

"Will we go on a plane? A boat?"

To uproot a whole family and move them across the Atlantic is a challenge and an adventure. As our family had grown, and needed more space, we had moved and changed houses from time to time, but always within the west coast of Sweden. This move was going to be very different, a move to a different country. A new continent. A new language.

I knew my husband, Lars, was doing well at work, and that it was a big deal for him to be in charge of the US division of his company. I was proud of him, but also a bit anxious. I was just forty years old (Lars was forty-two) and it was the first time we would move our five kids so far, to what seemed like another dimension. Little did we know then that this first major move would turn out to be far from the last.

As the children chattered away in excitement around the dinner table, I wondered how my own life would change. What would I do all day when the kids were at school? Most of all I worried about my English-language skills— they were not at all as good as I wanted them to be.

Today most Swedish children speak English fairly well. They learn it in school, but it's also probably thanks to television. In Sweden, when our children were young we had just one TV channel. Whatever was on, the kids watched, no matter what language was being spoken, Finnish, French, Hungarian, English. In Sweden we subtitle everything, instead of dubbing, so most kids back then learned English from TV shows such as *Columbo*, *The Rockford Files*, and *Scooby-Doo*. Today, with hundreds of channels, Swedish kids speak English almost perfectly.

So, when we arrived in the United States in the 1970s the oldest children could, thanks to television, speak and understand English reasonably well.

Youngest Jane had not started school yet. That spring, prior to our move, Swedish television aired a program for anyone interested in learning sign language. Jane loved the show and sat in front of the TV set as if she were glued to the floor. I believe she was worried about moving to a new country and not being understood. Perhaps she thought that at least she could communicate with the deaf kids at her new school. Unfortunately, none of us knew that English sign language is different from Swedish.

When I went to school in the 1940s, I had a lovely schoolmistress who taught us English. She looked a bit sullen, but if you studied her carefully you would notice that she had the friendliest eyes, filled with curiosity. Her name was Gertrud. That was not a very common name at that time. She was the first Gertrud I ever knew.

Gertrud had long hair, which she tried to keep in order with several combs that kept falling out, perhaps because she was very lively and moved around a lot. We always longed for her classes, especially those of us who had a hard time sitting still (who didn't?), because during her lessons we were allowed to move around too.

When her class started we all had to stand up next to our desks, thus forming a line. Then she asked us to walk slowly in our lines around the classroom. At the same time we softly murmured in English:

"I am,
you are,
he, she, it is,
we are,
you are,
they are!"

Gradually she encouraged us to increase our walking speed, and volume. Gertrud sat on her desk and kept pace by waving her pointer. Sometimes she would point at some-one who did not keep the pace or did something else wrong. Such fun we had! I think she enjoyed it as much as we did, and when the class was over we were stomping and scream-ing our grammar lessons. Her method really worked; her lessons are just about the only thing I remember today from the classes I took at school.

Learning languages isn't my strong point. This I realized on our first day in the United States when I had to buy gas. At that time, you did not have to leave the car to pump your gas. You just sat behind the wheel and waited and very soon the attendant showed up and said:

"Ma'am?"

Confusing our metric system and adapting to the Ameri-can way, I said:

"Please give me forty gallons."

This is actually about 340 liters! No wonder the poor attendant looked puzzled.

My oldest, Johan, who usually knows what to say and when to say it, laughed out loud and explained in embar-rassment:

"Mom, next time, just say, 'Fill it up.'"

Another time when I could not handle the language prop-erly was when we moved into our little terrace house in Annapolis. It was newly built; we were the first family to live in it.

One early morning I realized that there was a large puddle of water on our kitchen floor. I managed to get hold of the caretaker and handyman of the terrace houses. His name was Bob; he was a short and friendly man but always seemed to be in a great hurry.

"Please, Bob, help me; we have a large poodle under our kitchen table!"

Bob came running as fast as his legs could carry him. When he arrived, he wanted to know if he should call the dogcatcher.

I didn't have a clue what he was talking about.

A dogcatcher?

I showed Bob the poodle. And he burst out laughing.

"That, Mrs. Magnusson, is a puddle."

I have never confused the two again.

One Sunday morning a strange and rare thing happened: we woke up late and found that the entire family had nothing on the agenda. No excursions, no sports practices, no tournaments, no birthday parties or meetings to take part in.

Our home was shaping up nicely after the transatlantic move, so we were no longer stressed about unpacking boxes and settling in. My husband and I just lay in bed listening to the silence and enjoying it. For a minute.

Boys above the age of twelve sleep like stones. Deeply and perhaps forever, if you don't wake them. We had three sons; from their bedrooms there was no noise at all.

Our two daughters shared a room and we could hear their murmurs as they built a doll's house from some of the giant, now-empty moving boxes. It was a very nice project that kept them occupied for hours every day. We loved seeing how they used items that we had never seen in Sweden; a plastic tomato holder from the supermarket became a toy bed—things that seemed like trash to a normal American family were treasures to the girls. They invented new uses for empty matchboxes, pieces of textiles, bottle caps, muffin holders, pipe cleaners, and postcards.

The fuzz from the clothes dryer filter was something new and fantastic. We had never seen a clothes dryer before, and the girls made all kinds of amazing toy stuff from that lint: mattresses, cushions, wigs, anything. With the help of scissors, paper, and glue, my daughters turned out some rather nice creations. My husband and me, we also felt happy as we heard our little "angels" speaking in English to each other.

"Ah, they are learning so quickly!"

Then we heard the tones of the girls' voices changing. We could hear them getting annoyed with each other. Our little angels became louder and louder, almost aggressive. Then, suddenly, there were not enough words in their new English vocabulary. I knew the new language certainly had a lot of bad words and insults—my daughters had just not learned them yet. So they switched back to Swedish now and started yelling stuff like: "*Dumbom* [blockhead]*!*," "*Gris* [pig]*!*", "*Jävla skitunge* [damn brat]*!*"

For just a second my husband and I thought, How will this end? What will happen when American kids start picking on our daughters? How will they defend themselves? Should we teach the little girls how to curse and insult each other in English?

We didn't have to worry long, though: pretty soon our lovely little "angels" had mouths like sailors. I will not quote them here, but Lars and I laughed at their sturdy new language. They would be safe at school.

. . .

We are a big family, but I think, out of all of us, learning English was hardest for me. I made many mistakes and our children were quite amused by my linguistic somersaults. Sometimes, though, I think it could also be a bit embarrassing for them.

It was Sunday; Tomas had his birthday party. I think he was turning fourteen. It was a lovely sunny, but cold, winter day. All the children, his siblings and friends, were skating on the creek near our house. We prepared hot chocolate with whipped cream and cinnamon rolls for them, and when they came back to the house everybody was quite hungry and red cheeked. When they had taken the edge off their hunger there was still time to dance in their winter socks for a while before the party was over.

Most of the guests lived fairly close and could walk home, but the son of the headmaster of the school Tomas attended, who was one of his best friends, lived too far away to walk, so the headmaster came to pick up his son. When he arrived, he politely knocked at our door. At that time both parents and children had great respect for teachers and especially for headmasters, and no one wanted to look foolish around them.

Of course wanting to be welcoming, I offered him my Swedish cinnamon rolls.

As he munched, I asked the headmaster:

"How do you like my buns?"

The kids tried not to explode into laughter, but their stifled giggles made me suddenly embarrassed. Tom looked mortified.

Without missing a beat, the headmaster smiled in a friendly way and said:

"Mrs. Magnusson, your cinnamon rolls are really delicious."

When you move to a new place it takes a while before you discover what it offers that can amuse your children, to keep them occupied when they want to do something other than going to school or doing their homework. Our boys quickly discovered that we lived quite near two cinemas and whenever they had free time they always wanted to go there.

One time Tom invited out a girl from another grade. She was one of the daughters of Jane's beloved schoolteacher and Tom wanted this girl to join him to see a movie starring Peter Sellers. It was *The Return of the Pink Panther*. What Tom did not know was that in the United States at that time some parents still expected that if you invited a girl out you also had to bring a chaperone. I was asked by the girl's parents if their daughter would be chaperoned, so of course I promised to go with the children. I thought it was a little bit strict.

Anyway, I had already seen this movie and loved it. Therefore, I could not keep myself from starting to laugh long before every joke started. There are a couple of scenes that are so funny I can barely even write about them now, fifty years later. Can you imagine what I sounded like in that movie theater, guffawing loudly, tears flowing, bent over from laughing cramps? I was a mess. Not only had I asked his headmaster if he liked my buns, but now I was sitting a few feet from the girl Tom was trying to impress and I was laughing like a madwoman. Poor Tom.

I didn't get any more chaperoning jobs.

One day I noticed that one of the nearby cinemas was showing a movie that I felt sure that everyone in my crowd of children could enjoy, despite their different ages.

The title was *Alice in Wonderland*. I had read Lewis Carroll's wonderful book at least two times and loved it. Our family trooped over to the theater. I got in the ticket line while my kids played on the sidewalk.

The line in front of the box office looked a bit different from what I had expected. Not a single child. Mostly single men. And the line was long.

When I finally reached the ticket counter the seller said in a very discreet, low voice, almost a whisper:

"Ma'am, I am very sorry to inform you that I doubt your children will appreciate this version of *Alice in Wonderland*."

When I looked more carefully at the advertisement on the wall beside the counter, I realized that all the actors in the film seemed to be naked. And in bed with one another.

"Come along, children! It is sold out."

I took them to see *Bambi* instead. Not the pornographic version. I thought my children had forgotten about the incident—but they show no mercy. They still talk about *Alice in Wonderland* today, almost fifty years later.

Time passed. My English wasn't getting any better. Not having a work permit, I stayed at home by myself all day, painting, cleaning house, gardening. In many ways they were wonderful days.

When the kids came home from school, we spoke Swedish. When my husband came home—more Swedish. The aerobics class I went to in the late mornings wasn't made for conversation: What should I say to the woman jumping around next to me?:

Nice leg warmers?

These women were there to work out, not chat with a random Swedish woman with awful pronunciation and no vocabulary.

I racked my brain and then finally realized that to improve my English and learn more about American culture, I should start volunteering.

In the 1970s, in Annapolis, our three youngest children went to a school that encouraged parents and friends to help with different school tasks if they had spare time or if they had special skills they wanted to share.

I shouldn't have been surprised they sought help, as the school itself was housed in a number of more or less dilapidated but adjoining farmhouses, which needed constant work.

Parents who were carpenters could repair broken chairs, door handles, or windows that were hard to open. Artist parents painted the kindergarten building with wild animals and characters from children's books. Some parents serviced the typewriters and others organized bake sales, parties, and after-school classes. The list of things that needed care was endless. It was a warm and kind community.

Every Monday, I volunteered to take care of the school's library for the younger children. Not all human beings look forward to Monday mornings, but I sure did. This was a lovely way to start the week. I so enjoyed being together with these small creatures. They were always so friendly, curious, and full of energy. Even better was that their energy was very contagious. I, too, felt energized when the day was done.

Sometimes when they were not feeling friendly or curious or full of energy, they just needed to be comforted. Maybe they would come sit on my lap for a while and talk.

This library was a simple and cozy room entirely painted light blue. All the tiny chairs that furnished the room were light blue too, and the table had such short legs that we could use it even if we were sitting directly on the floor, which we sometimes did when there weren't enough chairs to go around (probably because some carpenter parent had taken them away to be fixed!).

The first to arrive at my Monday library session were the third graders. They took care of themselves quite well, which gave me time to reset the library stamp with the proper date, pre-stamp all the little library cards, and even drink a cup of coffee before the first and second graders arrived. They were all so sweet and full of enthusiasm. Some of them knew exactly which book they wanted to borrow, but unfortunately, they did not know the title of the book. Nor did they remember the name of the author. It could be quite tricky.

Sometimes they put their chubby little hands on my arm and tried to explain and explain and explain. Some were a bit anxious and had forgotten their books at home, while a cocky little boy who had already chosen his new book and had it stamped started to climb the shelves.

When all the children had chosen their books and had them stamped, I would read them a story. Just a short one. But even if the story was short, it seemed almost impossible to get to the end of it. Everyone wanted to tell their own stories of the similar things happening to them. Very often the children's own stories were so fantastical that any need I had for imaginative stories or fairy tales was satisfied. Or at least until the next Monday.

A little girl told us about when her dad knocked down her granny with his car in the garage. Another little girl was very proud to tell us how she helped her mother buy a bra that was bigger than the little girl's head. And another told us how her dog recently gave birth to nine puppies and how much work this meant for her and the whole family. Hers was one of the stories that got the most reactions: her classmates had so many questions, and everyone wanted a puppy of course. The children's stories used such simple words that I could follow them easily and oftentimes I even learned a few new words, thus expanding my vocabulary.

But these happy and instructive moments would soon come to an end, as it was time to close the blue library again after yet another wonderful Monday.

"Thank you, Mrs. Magnusson, thank you," said the children.

Someone added:

"Mrs. Magnusson, you have such a funny accent!"

Then they ran away to other important activities and the little blue library became very quiet again.

I sighed with relief when the children had left: my daughter was one of those students in the first grade class. I was grateful for every Monday that passed without her proudly telling her classmates how I had taken her and her siblings to watch a porn film.

I still continue to volunteer, here and there, and have been doing so ever since Annapolis.

In Singapore, where we moved in the late 1970s, I painted sets for high-school theater productions and for the elaborate synchronized swimming shows the school put on there. It was so much fun, but it was hard work. Just try dragging around a life-sized replica of a gilded Chinese temple in ninety-three degrees of humid tropical heat. In Singapore, at that time, there were a lot of poor families, so we organized food drives and collected cans of food and bags of rice to distribute. When boat people started arriving from Pol Pot's gruesome war in Cambodia, we gathered food for them too.

I say "we" because there were lots of women's organizations in Singapore that took pride in helping out. Many of the expatriate wives had left their jobs at home to accompany their husbands on their assignments, without work permits. Volunteering felt like a worthwhile, wonderful way to spend the days. I remember we made an international cookbook that we sold, giving all the proceeds to mothers in need.

I don't have as much energy now, but I help seniors learn how to email and use the internet. When they successfully send their first email, I see a glow in their faces that reminds me of the little blue library. Inside I feel the little-blue-library warmth too.

I understand that not everyone can afford to spend their time volunteering. We have never been very rich, but we have not been poor either—so I feel it is my duty to help out. Also, I've met so many nice people while doing it; some even became lifelong friends.

My mother-in-law was a lovely woman. But toward the end of her life she could be quite a handful at times. I remember her calling me up and complaining how lonely she was. I sympathized with her, but as I was in Annapolis, on the other side of the Atlantic from Gothenburg, there really was nothing I could do. Instead I advised her:

"Why don't you get in touch with a children's hospital or kindergarten and offer to read stories for the children?"

She never complained again.

Right now, spring is around the corner. I look out the window and long to get started with my gardening. When you are my age, it is important to fill your mind and days with stuff to do: planning, helping, thinking, and moving around as much as you can.

Unfortunately, my volunteering these days is limited to spring, summer, and autumn. So, the winter seems dull and endless. I hate it. Next winter, I have decided to start reading stories to children again.

TAKE CARE OF YOUR HAIR—
IF YOU HAVE ANY

Nobody wants to be in pain. Most people my age who are still active have, or have had, pain somewhere. Many have had knees, hips, and other bones and body parts replaced. They have labored with pain, suffered through rehab, and emerged very grateful that life has become so much easier and better afterward.

I had surgery for cataracts a couple of years ago. Before the surgery I found myself worrying a lot:

Will it hurt?

Will I have to be sedated?

What if I go blind?

Can I get to the appointment alone?

And on an entirely different level, my questions became worryingly existential:

Why am I saying "alone" instead of *on my own*? Do I feel alone? I have always enjoyed getting by on my own, haven't I?

Like a snowball rolling down a high mountain with nothing to stop it, the questions kept piling up in my head. Every thought turned into another problem, a new worry—all causing ever more anxiety.

A good friend reassured me by saying impatiently, "Get a grip! At least it's easier than having a child."

How we experience our fears is ultimately individual.

But really, I had worried unnecessarily. I got to the appointment alone, or on my own. I sat down in the waiting room, was given a sedative and some drops in the eye that needed to be fixed. That was the extent of the anesthesia. I waited for a while for it to kick in before I could go to the treatment room. There I had to lie down on an operating table while the doctor calmly and with a pleasant voice told me what he was doing:

"I'm removing the lens now."

Or:

"Now I'm putting a new one back in."

Or:

"Now I'm cutting your head off with a hedge trimmer."

The doctor now had a long beard that dragged on the floor, a little party hat from Tiffany's in sterling silver, and rotating ears. Even a little anesthesia can have a huge effect.

I kept still until he told me that he was finished and I could go sit in the waiting room again. Through the waiting-room window I saw the world slowly shift and change colors and shape. My eyesight had been slowly degrading for so long that I hadn't really noticed it. Now everything bloomed—in the middle of winter. The waiting room, the old ladies sitting across from me (no doubt waiting to meet Dr. Rotating Ears), the crisply patterned linoleum floor. The snow on the trees outside.

After about half an hour of sitting and gawking in amazement, I was allowed to go home. My vision was still a bit fuzzy; I had been warned that this was normal after the procedure. I had been told in advance that I should wear sunglasses to protect my eyes after the surgery for a few days. Even though I doubted that I risked being blinded by the dim winter light, I had dug up my finest pair of sunglasses and given them an extra polish. I was ready to catch my regular bus home and put my sunglasses on before I stepped outside. There I sat on the bus in my huge dark glasses, in the darkening afternoon, with the bright world outside. I felt like Greta Garbo—she did grow up in these parts after all! I had come and gone on my own.

Like Greta Garbo, I was happy to be alone.

When I finally got home, I noticed that all the colors in my home were different. They were stronger, deeper. A morning robe I had previously thought to be gray now had a soft purplish color—lilac. Amazing, and how exciting!

I felt compelled to walk around in my apartment and look at all my things like I hadn't seen them before. The plants, the paintings, the bookshelf, my red coat—everything seemed cleaner, fresher, yes, happier somehow. It was as if a coat of dust had been lifted. Even in the grayness of a Swedish late afternoon, all was newly vibrant to my eyes.

It felt incomprehensible that I, who had spent an entire lifetime working with colors, painting, and art, hadn't noticed that I had lost such a precious ability—the ability to see colors correctly, in all their nuances. It was a relief and a joy, as if I had been given a completely new power. I was a superheroine. "Wonder Woman" might be pushing it, but that's how I felt.

Then I went into my small bathroom and looked in the mirror. That, unfortunately, was less fun. Or rather: *it was a shock*.

In my heart I'm still twenty-five. My bad eyesight had helped me believe that, physically, I still looked fifty-five. Now came the truth: I had no idea that I had so many wrinkles! It was unpleasant at the time, but today as I write this at eighty-six, I'm even wrinklier. I am used to looking old now, and I would never trade my great new vision for the old, distorted image of myself. There are other ways of keeping young.

A lot of people seem to think that wrinkles can be fixed, but I don't think that's for me. I've seen too many people who suddenly look like they have been strapped inside a skin a couple of sizes too small, whereas others look swollen.

Plastic surgery does not make you look younger—to me it just makes you look like you have had plastic surgery. Which is fine if this is what you desire. Maybe I'll change my mind when I am 102 and my eyelids are so droopy my vision is once again impaired, but I don't think so at this point.

As she aged, my beautiful mother would look in the mirror and say, "Ugh, I'm a mess!"

And my mother-in-law used to say, "Lord, I look completely exhumed!" She who had been one of the prettiest girls in Gothenburg, with the boys lining up to ask for her hand. As she'd aged, in her eyes, my mother-in-law had come to think she had become unattractive—when in reality she hadn't. To the rest of us, a patina of warmth and a well-lived life shone visible in her face. That said, she never had surgery for her cataracts, thank God: she probably wouldn't have coped well with suddenly seeing herself as a raisin.

I feel—blessed as I am with a good head of hair—that it's more important to take care of your hair. No one's head of hair can be truly great if you are over eighty; it will have most likely thinned and lost its luster, and often lost its color too. But if you care about your appearance—which I do—then your hair is a better workplace than your face.

Most women my age cut their hair short—it is practical, I guess. And while I am all for practicality, I also must admit to some impractical vanity. While I can accept—even love—a bit my wrinkles—I don't like the shape of my face when my hair is short, so I keep mine shoulder length. It is not magic and it is some work; I comb, wash, and blow-dry it a lot. I never leave the house with "bed head." I am blessed with a good head of hair. If you are not, there are always nice wigs and dyes, masks, and conditioning treatments that can help to add interest and texture to our ageing, graying hair. If you do have good hair, grow it out and look for a nice blow-dryer or curling iron. You can be old and still have nice hair, making you look lovely.

I once saw a film where a woman talked so sensibly about how much she admired the strength of her own body—but I cannot for the life of me remember the title of the film. I think about her words when contemplating my own arms and legs and everything. My thoughts go something like this: My body has borne five children, plus one who didn't live. This body has died and it has awakened. This body has sheltered me in storms and baked an unholy number of cakes. This body has laughed and planted gardens, worn gloves, and loved. I will never put a knife to it for being wrinkled.

To me when I looked in the mirror after the cataract surgery that day, many of my wrinkles were new, but everyone I knew had already seen me with them. They were more used to the way I looked than I was! No one had been unkind to me because of the way I look and I've never really been horrified by the wrinkles on others either. If others had gotten used to looking at me, then surely I could get used to looking at myself. You must get used to it, unless you depend on your looks for your career or your joy. Hinging your life on looking young is such a bad idea.

If we laugh and try to have as much fun as possible each day, we'll get laughter lines instead of bitter crow's-feet. To laugh is more important and probably more effective than taking pills that might make us happy. But of course not everyone has something to laugh happily about.

When I have difficulty on dull, dark days finding anything to laugh about, I remember one thing that always
makes me choke with laughter.

A few years ago, I hosted a luncheon at my home. One
of the guests was a man who used to be my teacher in art
school. He had been a lot older than me then, and now he
was really, really old. He brought some films from a ski trip
our class had taken almost six decades before and wanted to
screen them to remind us of happy memories.

He had brought his projector with him. He looked for
an electrical outlet and, unfortunately, could only find a
rather inaccessible one in a corner behind a curtain. As
my old teacher was fixing the connection, he accidentally
knocked his head against the wall and then got tangled up
in the curtain and as he worked to get out of the twistings of
the curtain the whole arrangement came crashing down on
him with him still inside. He was unharmed, but the vision
of him, a curtain ghost waving his arms to get free, had our
old art-school class laughing so much that we almost forgot
to watch the ski movie. Once we freed him, our teacher
couldn't help laughing too.

Sometimes I wake up in the middle of the night and start laughing out loud at the memory of my art teacher, in a curtain toga. It was such a successful luncheon. I am sure that I got at least one more wrinkle from our laughing that day.

Once you have turned eighty, it's important to have the right sort of wrinkles. Even more important, though, is to start laughing early enough to spend more time laughing than frowning. If your wrinkles point upward, you will look happy instead of merely old.

TREAT LITTLE CHILDREN, BIG CHILDREN (AND GRANDCHILDREN) AS YOU WANT TO BE TREATED

Spending time with the young is good for anyone getting older; the best thing is that it gets easier: the older you get, the more and more people younger than you there are.

But within the group of younger people, perhaps my favorite is the very young, let's say children under eight. Not toddlers, but children old enough that they can at least (sort of) put sentences together.

When I was a teenager, I was determined never to have children. I do not know why; I simply thought they were annoying and whiny and completely unnecessary wastes of time. Thankfully, I changed my mind. Little did I know then that I would end up with five children and seven grandchildren.

Spending time with and talking to small children is really so fun and enriching. They have an unpredictable nature and a way of looking at things that you cannot even imagine, that you can never anticipate. Once I had small children of my own, I seemed to be surprised every day by what popped out of their mouths.

Traveling with children became a particularly enjoyable experience for me: children see everything with inexperienced, unspoiled eyes. Their comments can be unexpected and strange, and sometimes very funny.

My mother-in-law once told me about a long train journey she made with my late husband, Lars, when he was maybe four years old. At the time he looked like a little curly-haired angel. The train just kept going and going and baby Lars was terribly bored. After a long silence without anything interesting to look at, they passed a very large red barn.

In the countryside at that time, houses did not have indoor plumbing and hardly any had flushing toilets. Instead one used the outhouse, a tiny little house, always painted a special red color—*falu rödfärg*. It is a cheap paint, almost the color of bricks, which is why it became so popular. Way back in the day it was fancier to have a brick house than a wooden one. So, all wood house owners painted their houses to look like bricks.

Anyway, baby Lars had seen an outhouse before, but being a city child, he had never seen a barn. Baby Lars pointed at the barn:

"Vilket jävla stort dass!"

What a damn giant shit house!

This was 1936. My mother-in-law was mortified. She gave him an apple out of her purse to shut the little boy up. He munched and ate. After a while, the apple caused bowel movements in Lars's small body and a loud fart exploded. My mother-in-law was hugely embarrassed, but Lars didn't really know what had just happened. Over the din of the noisy train he yelled:

"Hostar stjärten?"

Is my ass coughing?

Being with my own children when they were young, I got better at knowing what they liked to do and what they were able to do.

When I had to take care of other people's children or grandchildren, it got a little trickier. Can they run on narrow bridges without falling into the water? Can they swim? They can certainly climb a tree, but can they get down when they discover how high they have climbed? Can they cross a street without causing a traffic jam?

In Sweden summer was so loved and awaited. As recently as the 1960s and '70s all kids up until maybe school age—seven years old—ran around naked all summer. No clothes, no shoes, nothing. That is, if you lived in the countryside as we did.

Today you would certainly think twice before letting your naked five-year-old out of the house, but no one thought anything of it then. In fact, people thought you were strange if you put swimsuits on your children:

"Whatever for? What have they got to hide?"

Today we put bikinis on toddlers. It is the natural thing to do.

But I remember when we moved to the United States and my younger daughter (six years old) refused at first to wear a bathing suit. As a result, she was not allowed to go in the water. It was a hot summer. She longed to swim. Finally, she agreed to wear a bikini. As she had never worn one before, she couldn't really handle the garment: the straps kept coming off; the top flopped down. She didn't care, but everyone else did. She was teased. She hated that bikini.

The year before we left for the United States, this same little girl, who loved to be naked and loved to dance, had seen a documentary on Swedish National Television that made quite the impression. It must have featured naked girls dancing. A few days later my husband and I hosted a dinner party for some important people. We were having cocktails and introducing our five children to the guests. They asked my little chubby five-year-old daughter what she wanted to be when she grew up:

"A stripper."

The guests fell apart in laughter and couldn't wait to hear the future plans of the rest of the kids. It seems all of them watched too much television—even though we just had one channel.

My son must have seen a show about people who stayed in bed all day, didn't have to do a thing, and were fed and taken care of by lovely women in uniforms. "And what do you want to be, young man?"

"A patient."

Now even my grandchildren are grown-up. They are young adults and it's so wonderful to be with them when they have time, even if they no longer blurt out funny, unexpected things. Instead I get to hear about all the exciting things they have in store. About schools, jobs, parties, hobbies, friends. And also about worries, joys, future prospects, and dreams.

So, how do you keep young people around you?

There is one very important rule—treat them as you want to be treated.

I know I have heard this somewhere before, but really.

Don't tell them about your bad knee, again. Don't guilt-trip them about not calling enough.

Just ask them questions. Listen to them. Act interested even if you are not.

Give them food and tell them to go enjoy their lives.

If you do these things, they will keep calling and visiting.

They will equate your place with a good place. Especially since their parents probably have less time than you do to talk to them.

DON'T FALL OVER
AND OTHER PRACTICAL TIPS
FOR GRACEFUL AGEING

Eyes, ears, yes, all our organs, are of course worn down after their years of service. I notice I've become slower and when I make the effort to push the pace beyond my natural speed I get very tired and often have to rest a bit, which, of course, doesn't speed things up at all.

If I'm out walking and suddenly feel tired, I usually take a pause and try to find something to look at for a while: a kid in the playground making a sand castle, a tree in full flower, a magpie hopping around—just a short break to collect myself before I carry on.

I've listened to my wise children and other friends and have had thresholds, small carpets, and anything else easy to stumble or slip on removed from my apartment. Yet a couple of months ago, I fell. *Splat!* There I lay all of a sudden, facedown on the floor, without any real meaning or purpose.

Falling down did hurt, though, and I couldn't get up. Of course, I should have pushed the alarm button that was strapped to my arm, but no. This will surely pass, I thought. I will be fine by tomorrow. So, I dragged myself to my bed and managed to climb in. A few hours later, I was not feeling any better. So, I finally pushed the alarm alert button I was wearing on my wrist. In no time at all, a young man came on the line from some senior-services-alarm-button-dispatch-office. He immediately called an ambulance to come get me. And then the wait began. . . .

It seemed there were no ambulances.

One winter night when our first son, Johan, was two years old, and fast asleep, my husband and I came up with the idea to make a film for him that we would show on Christmas Eve. We decided to let the family toys have the leading roles. The title of the picture was inspired by my husband's old stuffed animal that he had saved—imaginatively called *Gammelnalle* (Old teddy bear).

The opening shot is of Gammelnalle sitting on a shelf and pondering his existence. Suddenly he sees something out of the corner of his eye, turns his head, loses his balance, and falls to the floor. *Bam!* There he lies motionless. With the help of wires and tape, my husband and I were able to make the toy truck roll across the floor at great speed to help poor old Gammelnalle. Among our pile of toys there was also a really cute stuffed animal that looked like the cocker spaniel Lady of Disney's *Lady and the Tramp*. We cast her as the nurse and with the help of string and patience we got her to help Gammelnalle onto the truck. Off they went to some imaginary hospital, offscreen, in the kitchen.

Gammelnalle perked up, became healthy, and fell in love with the nurse dog. Everything ended well. And we were laughing ourselves to death making the film into the small hours of the morning. I recall we used an early form of do-it-yourself stop-motion and that there are plenty of shots where you can catch a glimpse of us being ridiculous. We also filmed a home video of showing little Johan the film. He was very confused about all the toys moving around. We used to screen that all the time at Christmas, and Johan's younger siblings would get a big kick out of seeing their big brother toddle around looking perplexed.

I thought about this when I myself had fallen over, just like Gammelnalle, even though I did not fall in love with my nurse and my ambulance service was much better.

My fall happened during the first days of the pandemic, early March 2020. Everyone was a potential carrier of the coronavirus. Everyone could kill you with a cough. No attendants, no visits, no going inside to help an old, fallen woman. The medical world was upside down. Nobody knew a damn thing. I phoned my younger daughter, who lives in the neighborhood. She came and waited outside my front door for four hours in order to let the paramedics in.

After a short stay at the main hospital I was moved to a lovely hospital a bit outside town, deemed to be covid-free.

There were four beds separated in a giant hall, one in each corner. The staff there was extraordinary. In my fall I had fractured my pelvis in two places. I was not very mobile at all. The staff helped me take a shower and meet a physio-therapist. I was seen by a kind doctor and it felt as if I was already on the mend, but I would stay the week there to heal. I was very grateful, but suddenly another doctor changed the plan and decreed that I was to return home posthaste. Maybe other patients were on the inbound and the doctors needed the bed? They didn't tell me.

Anyway, the notice came like a shock. The comfort, security, and kindness I had known at the lovely little hospital vanished in an instant.

When I got home, they put me into my bed. I lived alone and knew I couldn't take care of myself. My younger daughter once again had to act as my nurse, even though she had very little time. She was right in the middle of a project, but still she came through. She did whatever she could, helping me and taking care of my shopping, cooking, etc., as I lay there in bed.

Have you ever tried drinking from a glass lying down? Don't. There seemed to be no straws for sale anywhere. Many stores had been hit by an "anti-plastic-think," brought on by a sudden, but very laudable, sense of care for the environment. Finally, my daughter was able to find a hamburger place that shared some of theirs.

In any case, the situation was unsustainable. I became a grumbling, complaining patient and I didn't seem to be getting any better. As I had cracked my pelvis in the fall, just getting up to go to the bathroom was a painful, lengthy process. I didn't know what to do. My daughter helped as much as she could. Of course I could have asked for medical assistance at home—but there was a pandemic. I didn't want a lot of people running around in my apartment.

A good friend of mine had been living for a long time at a rehabilitation center after surgery. It had been very expensive and was not something that even the generous Swedish national health care system covers.

My solution was to get help from Japan, the United Arab Emirates, and Portugal. What is she talking about? you may be wondering. I promise I am not an aged member of a vicious global crime syndicate.

In truth, one of the unexpected benefits of writing my book about death cleaning was that countries around the world were also interested in the idea. A surprising United Nations of publishers had bought the rights to publish my book in their countries. Each one had paid a fee to publish the book and I'd been saving what I thought of as my winnings in an account for my children to use after my death. It now seemed I would have to use that money to pay for my own upkeep before my death. I felt sorry to be spending what I hoped to pass on to them but at the same time knew that by doing so I was saving them from being exhausted looking after me.

My aforementioned daughter/nurse called the rehabilitation center to see if they would take me and help get me back on my feet. It was such a relief when they welcomed me right away. My daughter arranged the transport and helped me pack some clothes, toiletries, and medicines. Not being able to do even the simplest things is very frustrating. For everyone involved.

In the beginning, I just lay flat on my back. Everyone was very kind and caring and helped out around the clock with almost anything I needed—retrieving a dropped pill on the floor, placing a pillow under my feet, charging the cell phone, helping me drink water.

After a couple of days, I was able to go to physiotherapy. Over the years, I've met many physiotherapists. If they are making a house visit, they usually come very early in the morning when all you want to do is remain in bed and pretend you are getting better. And if you are in a hospital, you have to walk long hallways with the therapist. Back and forth, back and forth. Sometimes we get sick of these hearty army sergeants, but I came to love them and was grateful to them. They worked so hard on getting me started again. Patient and cheerful, they tell us we're doing well, even though they know we want to tell them to leave us alone. Without them we would have never recovered; without them we might have just given up and dropped dead.

I'm back at my house now, recovered, using a walker. Thankfully, I was not at the rehabilitation center too long, so perhaps there will still be a few winnings from my international crime syndicate to pass on to my children.

I'm so happy with my walker, it's out and about in my home all the time. If you can believe it, sometimes I even misplace it in my two-room apartment. Then I feel anxious for a while, but at the same time I see it as progress. I mean, I must have left it in the other room because I could walk to the kitchen without it.

I've furnished my walker with a nice little basket, which more often than not is full of stuff that I plan to move from one place to another. Suddenly my small apartment can sometimes seem like a vast ocean, my little basket the cargo ship ferrying precious goods across to another continent, er, room. Though if I don't remember to always unload my cargo I may soon have yet another place to death clean: my walker basket!

The walker even has a small tray that serves as a rolling table for food and drink. Perhaps if I close my eyes I can imagine I am aboard a yacht enjoying a sunset drink and nibble with my loved ones in the South China Sea. Fending off pirates and cursing.

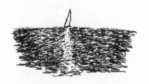

I call my walker Lars Harald, after my husband who is no longer with me. The walker, much like my husband was, is my support and my safety. I have a friend who, whenever she meets someone in town who has yet to see her walker, introduces it as her best friend. Another has endeavored for at least ten years to get rid of hers, continually angry over her inability to exist without it.

When I first saw my friends and contemporaries using walkers, I remember thinking it seemed unnecessary and was far too early for them to be relying on walkers. Now, after my fall, I know better!

If you are over eighty, or even if you are younger and feel a bit worried regarding your balance, you should get a walker. Because if you are over eighty, you must not fall. If you do, recovering is very hard work indeed. Save yourself the trouble.

And if you don't believe me about the value of a walker, then at least find a lovely, sturdy cane or stick that you can keep close as you wander across the sometimes-dangerous world of your living space. You never know what long curtains, or possibly even pirates, might be waiting to trip you up.

TAKE CARE OF SOMETHING EVERY DAY

We have always had animals of all kinds in our family. Cats, dogs, birds, fish, and mice. One of the boys even had a snake, when he was at college. For many years he was convinced he would become a veterinarian; these days he is instead an avid hunter, shooting wild boars all over Europe and stocking up the freezer. Animals bring joy in many different ways.

I have not been an animal owner for several years now. My home feels empty without a pet, I must admit.

But walking a dog in the pouring rain several times a day in a big city does not appeal to me. It was different when we lived in the countryside—walking around in nature was pleasant no matter the weather.

When we lived in the countryside my cats, Strimla (roughly translated as "Shred" in Swedish) and Klumpeduns ("Klutz" in Swedish), used to go with me when I went to pick up the mail a little ways down the road from our house. Or they would join me when I went out to pick mushrooms. They followed me with their tails straight up in the air.

Here in the city, an indoor cat would be nice and cozy. I would need to keep them inside, though; I can't imagine them following me down the street to the grocery with their tails in the air. I would worry they would wander off to explore and never come back. Would I have to lead them around on leashes? Cats on leashes I think are a bit bizarre.

Since living in a big city again, I have weighed the pros and cons of having another cat many times. They are very nice company, affectionate and cuddly. I've even gone so far as to think about the name that I might give this kitten. Some days I thought I might call it Caterpillar if it was a slow and fuzzy kind of cat who liked to curl up in a ball. Other days I thought I would call it Dogma if it was a more stubborn breed of kitten. Long ago I had a cat called Little Cat. When Little Cat had kittens, I kept one of them that was especially fluffy. I called her Lilla Päls—Little Fur. When Little Cat got old and died, my husband and I buried her in the shadow of a lovely pine tree in our yard. We were sad and missed her. Sadder still was her furry daughter, who curled up on her grave and lay there at length every day.

When you are older and particularly if you live alone, it is nice to have something to look after other than yourself. Even if you are in good health, looking after yourself takes so much time—you move slowly. To make your meals takes forever. Even just a simple *fika*—coffee and a sandwich or cake—takes forever to put together. Getting dressed and brushing your hair seems to take all morning, and once you have finished no one thanks you for doing it. I guess I could thank myself.

But with a pet, being kind to them, petting them, feeding them, connects you with another living being. While a pet is not likely to thank you either, they may still come to you for a cuddle. It feels good to have done something kind for something other than yourself; watching them grow and change each day is a bonus reward.

So, I have been imagining my little kitten curled up in my lap and the daily care of feeding and looking after it. In my dream, I easily forget I would have to lug the cans of food home and also clean out the kitty litter.

But in truth I can never really forget that even a little kitten would be a big responsibility. I also can't help but think about the day when I would no longer be able to take care of my cat. I'd need to arrange for someone else to give it food, water, and kindness.

I have now waited so long—and named so many imaginary kittens—that it is too late to have a kitten at all. Let's be frank—I would die before it. And even if I were not to die but just disappear for a few days to the hospital or more happily to see one of my children, what would happen? Who would look after Caterpillar?

I joke to my family about other animals I might get. Maybe a fish or an octopus? But an aquarium is a lot of work and I don't have the space. I also hear octopuses are like Houdini; if they can escape from anywhere, I am certain they can escape from an eighty-six-year-old woman who moves slowly. A hamster? A gerbil? A parrot? A parakeet? Who am I kidding? If I don't think I can look after a kitten, any other pet would be sheer insanity.

So, what can I look after and care for other than myself? I have read about care homes where old people were given little plants to look after. Apparently, the ones who had plants to look after and water every day lived longer. (When I read about this study, I wondered about the scientists who designed it—did they realize that by *not* giving some of the participants plants they were shortening their lives?)

From my own experience I agree with the findings of this study. While I have always been a gardener and still look forward to the springtime when I can get out onto the little balcony on my apartment to look after the outdoor plants, I also have a few plants by the window in my living room. Although they don't need to be watered every day, I make a daily habit of checking on them and watering them if they need it. Perhaps I prune a few branches or snip an unhappy, sickly leaf. Perhaps I even talk to my plants a little. Perhaps I tell them about the morning I have had. I notice small changes in them.

Given how slowly I sometimes move, just visiting them and watering them if they need it can take a while. I hope this doesn't sound too pathetic; I really do love the small daily habit of visiting with them and caring for them. Each day that I am alive and they are alive feels like a marvel.

Who will care for them once I am gone?

I don't know, but they are lovely plants and I feel sure someone will take them after me.

In the meantime, looking after them every day is something I look forward to. Having even a small thing to look forward to, something other than yourself to care for, is important whatever age you are.

Even if I can't have a kitten named Kathmandu, I am happy with my fern named Anni-Frid.

KEEP AN OPEN MIND

I hate it when things change.

When I was young, duvet covers had slits at the top that you could stick your hands into, grab the duvet by its corners, and easily slide it into the sheet. For some reason these slits no longer exist, and changing the duvet covers is a big hassle. Imagine if this were fifty years ago—when I had to change my family's seven duvet covers in one morning. I would have gone insane. If I purchase sheets today, I go vintage, and look for my old favorites with slits. The old kind don't have any stupid buttons either.

I love it when things change.

Just look at the sanitary napkins women use today. I am so impressed! The reusable menstrual cup is now distributed free of charge in many places, reducing garbage and making life easier for women in poor countries who can't afford pads and tampons or don't have running water. And look at today's pads! Finally, someone let a woman into the drawing room. These products are leakproof, perfumed; some are even eco-friendly and have wings. Oh, to be young again!

. . .

Although some changes are annoying, most of them are not. The important thing is to keep an open mind. The older you get, the faster things will seem to change. Faster and faster.

Even time itself seems to move faster. There is that funny phrase: "the older you get, the more it feels like breakfast comes every fifteen minutes." That gives me a laugh line, even though time passing will also give me a wrinkle.

When he was a teenager my son Tomas wanted to play the clarinet. My husband and I discussed it in detail. You do not go out and buy a clarinet every day, especially as children are fickle and might want to play the violin or the harp the next day. Also, the noise of a clarinet played by someone who is learning how to play it would no doubt be horrible. Our entire family would have to wear earplugs.

But my son was persistent and found a music shop where he could rent a clarinet. The rent would be considered an installment toward buying the instrument so that one day it would belong to him . . . if he stuck to it.

Playing a wind instrument is very difficult. Just to get any sound out at all can be very tiring. My son blew and blew and I saw his face turn blue. Finally, he and his rented clarinet produced a sound. Tomas's puppy, a basset hound named Jesper, sat beside his master and looked at him expectantly and full of terror. The sound that the clarinet made was far from beautiful. Jesper joined in and howled in pain, as if he thought he were in some jazz combo for people with no sense of pitch or musicality:

Ooouuuooauooowowo!

Jesper did this every time my son practiced. Tomas's clarinet aspirations were much worse than we had imagined. Our family had to suffer not only the sound of the clarinet but also the sound of Tomas's tortured hound.

One day when the racket was at a crescendo, I was downstairs in the kitchen preparing clam chowder, our favorite soup. Even in Maryland, we continued with our traditions and had soup and pancakes on Thursdays. I got the recipe from a nice neighbor who had brought us a giant pot of clam chowder when we arrived in Annapolis. Just to welcome us. What a nice thing to do! Clam chowder was somewhat similar to a fish soup we used to eat back in Sweden, so it was extra welcome when she brought it, as we had all been feeling a bit homesick.

Other neighbors had come with small plants or delicious cookies—at that time chocolate chip cookies were practically unknown in Sweden. They tasted like a delicacy from another world. The gifts of food helped us feel that we had friends nearby. Not at all like it is today when people really don't seem to want immigrants in their neighborhood. And not just in America. The world over.

Anyway, there I was in the kitchen stirring the chowder when I suddenly heard the strangest sound. It seemed to come from the upper regions of the house. I listened carefully. Now and then I heard the noise grow louder and then it would dim down again. I figured there must be something wrong with the pipes. To be on the safe side I called the plumber and rushed upstairs to try to locate where the noise was coming from. I held my breath and listened. It wasn't the pipes. My son had simply reached a new stage in his clarinet playing: he (and Jesper) no longer sounded like a tone-deaf music ensemble. They now sounded like the broken pipes of a haunted house. I rushed downstairs again to cancel the plumber.

My husband and I began to realize that this was perhaps what our future would sound like. Should we have a talk with Tomas, tell him this couldn't go on? Forbid him to play? No, of course not. We are open-minded; the kids must flourish. I still feel guilty; I have to admit that we perhaps didn't cheer him on like we did some of our other kids with their sudden new interests.

Needless to say, we were all quite happy when he gave up instruments and started to play American football instead. In rented football gear too. It felt almost magical to return the clarinet to the shop, released from its spell of cacophony.

Next, my daughter Ann wanted to learn how to ride a horse. She had discovered a place called Littlehales Stables not far from our house. One day she took her bicycle and went off to see if she could find someone there who could help her to realize her dream.

When a girl, almost a teenager, wants to start horse riding you can be quite sure that the idea is not going to disappear in the near future.

When Ann returned from her excursion, she was beaming. Not only did the stables have room for more riders; they also welcomed girls who wanted to use their spare time to help with the chores in the stables. If you worked hard, you could get more riding time as compensation. Ah, the beauty of free labor, the essence of America. Furthermore, her little sister would also be welcome. They had a tiny Shetland pony called Peanut that would suit the little sister well.

The little sister had never showed any interest in horses, but she was happy to go with her big sister, whom she admired deeply.

Unfortunately, little Peanut threw little Jane off right away. Maybe the pony was uncomfortable with someone on its back? Maybe Peanut was having a bad day? Maybe the saddle strap was too tight? Whatever the reason, and despite her little riding helmet, Jane got a minor concussion.

Humiliated and a little scared, I think, she never rode again.

But otherwise, Mrs. Littlehales was the perfect riding teacher. Ann loved being there, feeling more comfortable in a new country. Mrs. Littlehales taught the kids how to ride and jump but also how to take care of the horses, their harnesses and boxes. And the kids did indeed get their reward for all that free laboring—more time in the saddle.

Very soon Ann was spending all her time at the stables. She groomed and brushed and cleaned the hoofs. She braided manes. She cleaned out stables. Sometimes she was allowed to drive a small tractor to carry a bundle of hay into the stables. She was very happy with her new interest. But I worried. All the time.

Horses are so big. If they throw you off, you might break your neck, back, or leg. In the stable, a kick would damage you permanently. But I couldn't forbid my daughter from riding all those horses that she loved. But for all her teenage years, boy, did I worry about her and the horses.

In retrospect, things worked out ok. She rode with a passion for many years. Unharmed.

As an adult, riding at a stable in Sweden, she was thrown off. She was unharmed, but she rides no more. The benefit is that I no longer have to worry about her riding. I am grateful.

In the seventies, the equipment, helmets, and protective gear were really substandard in many stables. Now when I look at what my granddaughter wears when riding I really appreciate the changes. On her head she wears almost a motorcycle helmet. She also wears a back brace and leg protection. Horse riding is still a dangerous hobby—but at least people seem to understand that now.

Change and progress are great in this aspect. I would never say that horse riding was better in the good old days. Instead I am a bit ashamed that my little girls were allowed to ride without proper protection. It was hard to let them go to the stables. It was hard when they came home and smelled of horse shit. But I tried to keep an open mind. Then. And now.

When we were living in Singapore, my daughter Jane wanted to join a Bible study group. Some of her classmates were already members and the group was led by the mother of one of the girls. They were a merry and friendly lot and my daughter liked them very much. I thought this could be interesting for her, especially since no one in our family had much to add on the subject of Jesus.

One day every week I drove little Jane to the study group. The girls and the mother sat at a round table. They seemed to have a very good time discussing Jesus.

After some months the Jesus mother asked me if my daughter was allowed to be christened.

I answered:

"Jane is already christened."

"Yes, but then she was just a baby and she did not get to choose to do it herself."

True and right.

So, I asked my daughter what she thought. She said that she wanted very much to be christened or baptized, as they called it. I had seen people getting baptized in a small creek when we were living in Annapolis; it looked a bit strange but not too dangerous.

The ceremony was going to take place at the home of one of the girls; her house had a large pool. The events were arranged almost as if the baptism were a cocktail party—but with fruit juice. The guests all dressed nicely for the event. We mingled and chatted. At the edge of the pool a huge parrot with colorful plumage walked slowly back and forth. It had a ring around its leg, and the ring was attached to a chain that rattled. Every minute the bird croaked:

"Hello, hello, be quiet!"

I said nothing but felt deeply that I was part of a Fellini picture. David Lynch had not yet made his first film.

After a short while the priest, Mr. Lim, arrived accompanied by the others who were going to get baptized. In Swedish the word *lim* means "glue." I mused in silence about Mr. Glue getting stuck to things, or helpfully gluing broken china together in his spare time with just a touch of his sacred hand. Perhaps he was a mender of things, not just of human souls.

Mr. Glue and the soon-to-be-baptized were dressed in long white gowns. Together they got into the swimming pool very slowly and carefully, all still wearing their gowns.

The fabric of their holy attire was so dense that it took some time for the air to bubble out of their clothing. For a while the group in the water looked like big white balloons.

In this solemn moment after the white balloons had sunk into the water and my daughter was dunked into it, I thought I saw her smile. Maybe she was thinking, It is not every day you get dunked in a swimming pool, by a Mr. Glue, dressed as a white balloon, with a parrot walking around it and a bunch of expat parents drinking juice and parading around in 1980s cocktail outfits. That is at least what was on my mind. Maybe it was on her mind too; she's grown up to be a woman with a surreal sense of humor, though I think less belief in Jesus than she had back then.

We said thank you and good-bye to the host and hostess, the priest, and the friends of the parrot. As an unbaptized mother, I was a bit relieved to return to my more atheistic household, though once back at the house my daughter proudly showed her siblings the new Bible she had been given. One of her brothers said:

"Great, let's throw it on the fire."

That evening when I went to Jane's room to say good night I could hear her praying:

"Dear Lord, please save my damn brother."

Today, almost fifty years later, I realize I might have

been strict when I should have been more lenient, and soft when maybe I should have been a block of concrete. It is hard to raise five kids on three different continents. Most of the time I shot from the hip, making it up as I went along. There was no guidebook to help me find my way, and yet, today, the kids are all right. My eldest is past sixty. The youngest past fifty. Perhaps I shouldn't call them kids anymore. But to me they are.

In Annapolis, my two eldest sons, Johan and Jan, did not have any time for extracurricular activities. Their days in school became longer and their hills of homework grew into Kebnekaise, the highest mountain in Sweden.

Across the street lived a nice family who had two lovely daughters who were about the same age as our boys. What a coincidence and what luck! It did not take long before their studies were diluted with movies and games. And with tea and sandwiches or cinnamon rolls in our sunken living room.

A sunken living room was something we had never seen before we came to America. For us it was difficult to explain to our Swedish friends exactly what it was. A rectangle about four by five square meters was submerged approximately eighty centimeters into our living-room floor. It was the 1970s and naturally the floor was covered with a deep shag carpet—dark brown. Imagine a baby pool drained of water and dressed in a fur coat. We threw a lot of pillows in there and tried to keep bread crumbs and popcorn out of it. It was a perfect place to relax or have fun. For teenagers it must have been heaven.

My sons sometimes helped me in the garden. One time I asked them to dig a fairly big hole where I wanted to plant a white rosebush. I do not really know what happened, but suddenly they started to quarrel. Very soon they were fighting, throwing punches and wrestling. I got scared and feared for each of them. What should I do? To intervene in the fight was not a good idea, to slug them with a rake was even worse, and to cry for help was totally out of the question. I wasn't really in danger—and what would the neighbors think when I couldn't handle my own two sons?

Sometimes you get a sudden impulse that cuts through all your garbled reasoning. My mind opened up and in one second it seemed to take in my full surroundings. I grabbed the garden hose from its loop and in seconds I was spraying my beloved sons with ice-cold water. It worked. The two separated, shocked back to reality. The three of us burst out laughing. Falling over with laughter, actually. We saw our neighbors peek at us from behind their curtains, shaking their heads. We laughed even more.

A few months later it was October 31. Daylight savings had just set in. My watch said 7:00 p.m., but it felt like 8:00 p.m., as it was so dark outside. In fact, it was pitch black. And somewhere out in that darkness we could hear children laughing and yelling.

Our doorbell had been ringing and ringing since sunset. It was Halloween and since we had never before celebrated this holiday we were all curious, excited, and a bit nervous. In Sweden, in 1975, nobody had ever heard of Halloween, and we worried that we wouldn't get it right. We so desperately wanted to fit in. Today in Sweden, it is a different story. Everyone celebrates Halloween; it is almost a national holiday. Kids knock on my door and ask for candy. People dress up and go to parties. So much can happen in only ... forty-five years.

Back then, the people at our door were children of different sizes and ages, rigged out in costumes of all sorts of creatures and personalities. I really had to admire their inventiveness.

"Trick or treat!" they all more or less shouted when we opened the door.

We had been told to give a treat and not ask for a trick. The kids probably didn't really know any tricks. Besides, what if the trick wasn't very nice, or if the trick was very complicated and took an excruciating amount of time to complete? With a host of monsters, demons, and other oddities trooping to our door, we didn't have time for tricks. Only treats.

My sons Jan and Tom, were busy filling paper cones with sweets to give to the trick-or-treaters. In no time, they had to run to the store to buy more candy, as the first thirty-five cones they had prepared were almost gone. I guess that many children living on our street were curious to see the odd foreigners who had arrived in the neighborhood.

"Are they friends of ABBA?" Could the strangers with the funny language from another country be communists?

I don't think the hose incident on the front lawn helped our reputation much. A few nights after I had sprayed my sons with water and a few nights before Halloween we had a drive-by incident. Some drunk kids in a car threw bottles at our house and yelled:

"Fucking commies! Fucking commies, go home!"

This was 1975. Sweden was a socialist country and had been so for many years. In America at that time people were terribly afraid of communism—much like Swedes at the time were afraid of capitalism. I don't blame people for being suspicious. Some neighbors gave us soup; some didn't. Such is life.

At that time, we had our lovely basset hound called Jesper. He was forever stealing our next-door neighbor's dog's food. We overheard the neighbor complaining loudly that we had trained our "commie spy dog" to harass his fine American Chesapeake Bay retriever.

We laughed and said to ourselves:

"We wish!"

We'd never even managed to teach Jesper to sit.

While the boys gave out the candy, our girls were getting ready. I could hear them giggling.

Ann was dressed as an old man. She ran over to Judy, the girl next door, who was hard to recognize in a penguin costume. Jane and her friend Julie from across the street were dressed as conjoined twins. They wore one of my husband's huge sweaters with both their heads sticking out of the neckline. They also tied two of their legs together and got into a pair of trousers with three legs that I made from two pairs of worn-out jeans.

Today we know conjoined twins in reality often suffer terribly and this costume isn't a great idea. But this was 1975 and people thought differently. They were more afraid of communists than offending minorities. The twins moved forward with great difficulty and hobbled around the neighborhood together with another little girl dressed as a skeleton.

After a while I drove the conjoined twins and the skeleton to the governor's residence, which was located at the top of a hill in Annapolis. The governor and his wife were standing at the top of the stairs in front of the house's grand entrance giving away bags with sweets. Forty hollowed-out eerily carved and lit-up pumpkins illuminated the pathway up to the governor's porch. A spectral feast for our eyes. The whole scene looked magnificent on this very dark and spooky night.

The little skeleton squeezed my hand.

When you are over eighty, it is easy to be angry. There is new stuff all the time—new politicians, new countries, new wars, new technologies. Everything is in fact new and getting newer all the time. If you are over eighty, you have two choices—be angry or go with the flow. Please try the latter. To accept, even enjoy, the changes can be really fun.

When we were living in Singapore we were invited to a Chinese wedding. None of the kids wanted to go, but I tried to drag them along. This might be the only Chinese wedding in their lives. It wouldn't kill them. Only one came with me.

The bride was named Susan; she was a friend of mine I had met in a cooking class. For the wedding party she and her fiancé and a group of other newlyweds had booked a giant party venue, decorated in red and gold. Blushing, happy, exuberant couples in lovely Chinese silks took turns getting on the stage and being toasted by the immense crowd: "*Yam seng* [meaning "Cheers," literally Cantonese for "Drink to Victory"]*!*"

In Sweden we say "*skål*" instead of "cheers." *Skål* in Swedish is the same as "bowl." Many people want to think that *skål* is a modern word for "skull," that our ancestors the Vikings drank out of the skulls of the people they had slaughtered. This is not true. The Vikings were horrible and ruthless and did enjoy their mead, but to drink it out of a freshly chopped skull was not on the agenda. So they drank out of bowls and yelled, "*Skål* [Bowl]*!*" at one another.

In Sweden we have a number of unusual culinary delights. It seems like celebrity chefs come to our country every summer to sample *surströmming* live on camera. There is a certain moment—in August—when you open the can of *surströmming*—a rotted fish. You dress it in all kinds of condiments: onion, sour cream, wrap it in a special Swedish tortilla, and eat it in tiny bits. It is awful. Some people love it. I have tried it once. Never again.

At the Chinese wedding, we were seated at a round table

that held eight guests, a most auspicious number. We were the only non-Chinese people at the party and it felt as if we were treated with extra attention and care. There was a spinning tray in the middle of the table; with their chopsticks the six other guests at our table made sure to pick choice pieces of food from the many dishes to put on our plates, as is the custom with important guests. We certainly weren't so important, but it was lovely that they treated us as such.

In Sweden we call the fatty part by the chicken tail *gumpen*. We throw it into soup stock and don't eat it on its own. At this wedding, it was considered a prime morsel. Our table mates put the fatty little tails on our plates. We ate them dutifully. As we hoped for something else a bit more familiar to eat, they started grabbing more little tails from other tables. The *gweilo* (ghost people, i.e., us) seemed to love them.

It was a long night. It was a lovely night. It was a night of indigestion.

We were in Singapore for six years. So much happened. We had so much fun. We do not remember any night more clearly than this one, the night of chicken fat—the night of the *gumpen*—Gumpen Eve. A night we were treated like royalty.

The older I get, the more I find that I remember clearly all the things I said yes to, just when I was about to say no. I must admit I have not been open-minded all the time. I just wish I had been.

EAT CHOCOLATE

How great did hot chocolate with whipped cream taste when you were a kid? There you sat with all your friends on a snowy day or at a birthday party and you all had white cream mustaches.

Or when the family went skiing on a cold, sunny, crisp day during winter break. It was so lovely to drink a cup of hot chocolate while gliding along through the snowy woods. Skiing and sipping from a thermos: it gave you renewed strength to carry on, enough for the rest of the day.

Sometimes, at home, when my sister and I had a craving—we both had a sweet tooth—we would mix together sugar, cocoa powder, and some milk into a gooey concoction that was much too easy to finish all in one gulp. You never get too old for the taste of chocolate. I still find it deliciously tasty, but these days I much prefer it in the form of chocolate bars. Even better, you then don't have to clean up any mugs or mixing tools.

In my teens I suddenly discovered how easy it was to outgrow my clothes. I don't know if it was because I continued to eat chocolate—and anything else sweet that I could find—or it was just my hormones or the growth spurts of that age, but I began to find my continually shrinking clothes very annoying. It seemed as if every month I was asking my mother to let out the waists of my skirts or lengthen their hems. She made me do the sewing, which I didn't love to do.

After all the alterations, I began to try to eat a bit less chocolate and maybe just a little less of everything, but still I grew. I never developed anorexia or bulimia—terrible diseases that did not even have names when I was growing up—but it did lead to a lifelong sensitivity about my weight and perhaps a little too much awareness of my diet.

In my early twenties, when my future husband, Lars, started calling me *rundstycke*, I couldn't laugh along with him: where I am from *rundstycke* is the word for a bread roll, or a fluffy bun. I was determined not to be a *rundstycke*.

Pretty soon I knew the little handbook *The Calorie Guide* by heart. Maybe I'd be fine for Lars to call me something like *finsk pinne* (a long, thin cookie), but I was a bit concerned that he might not like to marry a fluffy bun.

Of course you can eat everything and lots of it, be round, beautiful, and happy. If I were a different person that might be completely fine, but wearing caftans is not my style.

Then (and now) I really liked to wear and enjoy the clothes I already had. I was also too lazy to always be using a needle and thread to readjust and alter my clothing. (In the 1940s and '50s when the world was still recovering from the world war, there were certainly not the endless amounts of cheap disposable clothes there are now.) At the same time I wanted to be able to eat well without having that stubborn little needle on the scale moving ever farther to the right.

Using *The Calorie Guide*, I discovered how I could eat my fill without outgrowing my clothes. It worked so-so, I guess. I got a bit tired of cucumbers, which, from what I understood, burned off more calories in the digestion than they returned to the body. But with *The Calorie Guide*, I did at least get better at math as I sat there at the kitchen table, trying to add up in my head all the calories I had consumed during each meal. Lars was pleased; he began to think I had a head for numbers and thus the ability to stay on top of household economies—a job I rather excelled at over the years.

After surgery a few years ago, I went to rehab to get back on my feet again. There I had the misfortune of being matched with a scratchy, rather unfriendly nurse, who thought I was much too skinny.

It was sometime after my dear Lars had died. While I didn't worry about him thinking I looked like a *rundstycke* any longer, my youthful days of cucumber salads were long gone. While skinniness certainly wasn't something I strived for—I'd long ago given away my calorie counter book, probably to a rummage sale—I had lost several kilos during my recovery from the surgery. Perhaps youthful vanity never really dies, so at first I was pleased when this nurse pointed out that I looked "skinny"... until she went on to say that she thought skinny elderly people look *very* gray and *very* lonely. She could have been a bit nicer, that nurse.

In the past, my friends and I used to joke that maybe the best way to keep our ageing, beginning-to-sag skin taut would be to eat second helpings of food so delicious that it would both fill us up and perhaps plump up our ageing lines. Reaching for another piece of cake, one of us would say:

"It will always fill out a wrinkle."

After my unfriendly nurse's comment, paying attention to what I ate was no longer a joke. Eating more became of vital importance; one does not have to be vain to not want to look *very* gray and *very* lonely.

But cooking for yourself and eating alone isn't fun. I think most people would agree with me about that. You might say the answer is to invite someone over, but it's not that easy to travel at my age, even just down the block. In our most recent, anxious times, that walk down the block to get to a meal in an enclosed space takes on a whole new terrifying meaning. Even with our current obstacles, I think that most people, even some as old as me, have found ways with particularly cautious close friends or family members to meet up on occasion, outdoors or at home. It is possible to keep a distance even at a set table and it is certainly more fun to cook up something good if you don't have to sit and eat it alone.

After I said good-bye to my unfriendly nurse and returned home, a really nice and friendly dietitian began to visit me weekly. She always brought a scale with her and she gave me no choice but to step up on it. She then ordered me to drink special nutritional weight-gaining drinks and gave me other sound dietary advice. As I put on weight, she came less and less frequently. I thought that was a good sign. I am beginning to think she may never need to come back. . . .

The hot chocolate and whipped cream of my childhood

left their mark on me and the mark gets deeper the older I am, which seems weird, given that the memory of those childhood times should get further and further away. The memory of that delicious chocolate returns to me. More and more I long for it. And these days with no calorie counter, no visiting dietitian, and no cucumber salad, my longing doesn't last very long. I just give in to it, to my desire for that chocolate.

In the months when I could not go outside, when visitors dropped my groceries outside my door, I always requested a supply of chocolate bars.

My relation to chocolate is now like in that film *Little Miss Sunshine* where Alan Arkin—bless him—plays the grandfather who starts doing heroin at age seventy-something.

What the hell, he thinks.

That is me with chocolate right now: What the hell, I think. I am eighty-six. If the chocolate doesn't kill me, something much less pleasant will.

Reaching for my chocolate bar, I think of those brave retired Japanese firemen and rescue workers who offered to enter the nuclear power plant of Fukushima after the tsunami disaster to shut it down and clean it up, even though they knew by doing so they were dooming themselves to deadly radiation poisoning.

But they thought, Let us in! We can do this! We know how to stop this disaster! We know how to make everyone safe!

They reasoned, Why make young people clean up this mess and get radiation poisoning? We are too old to die from whatever the Geiger counter says.

I guess they said, "*Nante kotta* [what the hell]*!*"

なんてこったい

While I am certainly not saying that my addiction to chocolate bars will contribute to my saving my nation from a tragedy, I do admire their spirit. When you get to be very old, sometimes there are days when all you can say is: "What the hell!"

There have been tons of studies done on the positive effect of chocolate on our circulation, heart, and brain. But chocolate is like red wine—for every study that tells you it will do good things for you, there is a competing study that tells you all the terrible things. Too much red wine causes elevated blood sugar levels, or elevated heart arrhythmia, or just getting very drunk. What the hell!

But life always seems to give you what you deserve. There is no escape: even in old age there are consequences for your decisions. My decision to eat chocolate bars as if I might live forever—or, more correctly, just no longer too concerned if I don't—seems to have earned me an allergic reaction. Now, whenever I eat my first little piece of chocolate for my daily dessert, something strange happens. I start sneezing. Sometimes aggressively—eight or nine times in quick succession.

But as soon as I stop sneezing, I reach for the next bit of chocolate. At my age it is really important to sometimes think, What the hell!

THE HABIT OF *KÄRT BESVÄR*

There's an idiom in Swedish—*kärt besvär*—that I quite love. I think it sums up many of the important things we do in life. And as one ages, it seems more and more that everything becomes a *kärt besvär* (sounds like "shairt bessvair").

The words break down to *kärt*, meaning "dear or cherished or beloved," and *besvär*, meaning "pain or sorrow," but it can also mean a burden or something that is a nuisance.

Paying your monthly bills might be considered a *kärt besvär*: they are an annoying obligation, but you are grateful that you have the money to be able to pay and can feel good crossing them off your to-do list.

Or a more heartfelt example might be looking after a sick loved one. Taking care of a sick person can be a burden, but being well enough to nurse them back to health is its own blessing, something to be cherished and something the sick person will also be thankful for, even if they never tell you.

The older I get, everything I do seems to be its own sort of burden—almost anything can now be physically or mentally difficult. There seems to be no other choice than to see each and every burden, every nuisance, every pain, as something that is also dear, something that I must find a way to cherish.

Two things that I apply my approach of *kärt besvär* to are my memory and the daily routines I stick to, to keep me sane and relatively healthy.

I'm sure it happens to all of us at some point: we think we are losing our memory or simply going crazy. Sometimes it can be that we feel we have too much to take care of, too much to do. But we can do much more—and remember much more, unless we have a terrible illness—than we believe we can. Sometimes it just takes a bit more time and patience with oneself and perhaps changing our approach.

The older we get, the more often our memories can play tricks on us. But having a good memory is wonderful, so I still try to have one. Not because I want to know train time-tables by heart, but remembering people's names is not only nice but also important. When I find myself searching to remember a name, it is a pain. When I suddenly remember it, it is a beloved joy.

I know that even by the age of forty it can become increasingly difficult to remember names. I remind myself of this often: Now that I am more than double the age of forty, why would it be so strange when I go to get something in the kitchen and once there I have forgotten what I was going to pick up? It's a bit annoying, but if I retrace my steps to where I began my journey I will soon remember what it was I was going into the kitchen to get. It was a nuisance to walk all the way back, but boy was I grateful that I remembered.

Many people claim that crossword puzzles and Sudoku are good for keeping the mind fresh. People also say bridge and other memory games force the brain to make an effort. I think those people are probably right, but I have never been very good with puzzles or card games.

But more than mental games, researchers claim that physical exercise is a must for the ageing brain. Physical exercise is important not only for our general well-being but also for coping better with stress, becoming more creative, and having a better memory.

A good friend once told me that you should never sit still for more than twenty minutes at a time. This doesn't work if you like going to the cinema—unless you are going to a short-film festival.

I read somewhere that the chair is our most dangerous invention—that more people die from unhealthy conditions that are exacerbated by sitting too much than by anything else. I don't know if that is true, but I try not to sit too much. I prefer to stand or to move around as much as my walker allows. I've even found a way to make doing daily exercise fun; at around 9:00 a.m. every day I follow along with a short and light gymnastic program on television. It is certainly *kärt besvär*: sometimes I can't believe my old body can move at all and it often aches. Yet I'm so grateful that I can at least—sort of—follow along.

Too much free time on your hands? Strange new shortened sleep patterns where you wake long before sunup wondering if you actually slept at all? These are other perils of ageing and challenges that are a daily battle.

The older one gets, the more one must find a way to make any routine a beloved routine, even if it is sometimes a pain.

My daily newspaper arrives every morning, then perhaps I reread books I'd forgotten I had on my bookshelves. Perhaps I imagine future hobbies I will take up. I use the phone a lot (my children can tell you . . .). I wash my clothes and my sheets and towels regularly. I keep my little apartment as tidy as possible; I am very happy my apartment is not bigger.

None of these activities are extraordinary, I know. You were expecting Swedish secrets, and yet I think the secrets of ageing well and happily are in finding ways to make your routines dear to you. I may not have a choice in how long they will take me to do or whether I will even be alive a few weeks from now, but I do have the choice to decide how to approach my daily life. Most days—not all days—I'm able to see my daily routine, my daily life, as *kärt besvär*.

WEAR STRIPES

I don't know why, but there is something strange about stripes, something almost magical.

A lonely stripe can be simply a line or just a stroke of a brush. A single stripe can point us in a direction but also can be limiting, yes, even mark a stop. Several stripes together can form interesting patterns.

I love stripes. Mostly lengthways but crosswise is also ok. I feel fresh and lively if I put on a striped sweater or dress. It's a timeless fashion that suits both men and women of all ages; it's graphic and bright, but also in control.

Stripes are sporty but not so sporty that you look like you are part of some training squad for Vasaloppet. Vasaloppet is a major Swedish cross-country skiing event for the really insane; it's the oldest cross-country skiing event in the world, in which skiers traverse ninety kilometers of frozen late-winter Sweden. The race commemorates one of our kings' fleeing from an invading Danish king. I doubt either was wearing stripes: I don't think they were in vogue in 1520.

Horizontal lines are said to be calming because they echo the simplicity of the horizon; I think I agree. Vertical lines on the other hand can sometimes feel a bit more oppressive, as if a gate or an elevator door slammed shut in front of your nose. But a stripe is a stripe in any direction.

As a little child, you are happy the first time a pen leaves an imprint on a piece of paper. Perhaps you drew a line. And perhaps you soon discovered that if you drew more lines you created a house, then more lines created a stick figure who might live in your newly drawn house. Unfortunately, I don't know how that same little child feels the first time they come in contact with a computer. But of course there are other discoveries to be made there. That feels comforting at my age.

Many artists have spent the greater part of their artistic careers painting lines. Fifty-one-year-old Swedish artist Jacob Dahlgren is one of them. He thinks of himself as a living exhibition for his artistic ideas and obsession with stripes. He has worn striped T-shirts for almost fifteen years now. His collection of striped T-shirts is vast. All his art is striped—it is fascinating.

A couple of years ago, I saw one of his exhibitions at the Andréhn-Schiptjenko gallery here in Stockholm. There was so much ingenuity and joy and everything was made of stripes! One large piece (roughly two by three meters big) looked very exciting, I thought, so I moved closer to it. There I discovered it was made out of tightly clustered wooden black and white coat hangers. From a distance it looked like they were all occupying the same space. It is hard to explain. It was striped. Most of the works were in bright, clean colors, and there was so much to see and be amused by.

Jacob Dahlgren has made many public artworks around Sweden. His work is represented in several museums around the world, including the Gothenburg Museum of Art. The popularity of his work is a testament to the fact that most people really like stripes.

Not being as mobile as I used to be, I take great pleasure in going to exhibitions online and visiting an artist in their studio. When I discovered Irish-born artist Sean Scully online, at first it took some time to understand his paintings and to understand why I loved his work. His specialty is large paintings with stripes painted in muted color tones, which he sometimes repaints endlessly. The other day I virtually peeked into his studio while he was working—amazing.

These two artists are each other's opposite: one uses stripes to communicate joy and playfulness; the other conveys a heavier, sometimes even somber beauty.

Throughout the centuries, striped clothing has been both hated and loved—it's played many different roles. Football referees used to wear black and white vertical stripes and were of course always hated. Prisoners wore striped uniforms. We would rather like to forget those connotations. But I don't mind remembering the beautiful dress with broad black and white stripes that our Swedish Queen Silvia wore at the Nobel Prize party in 1993. Nina Ricci designed that one.

I have a few striped dresses myself but none so glamorous as Sylvia's. These days I don't wear them, but I can't bear to give them away. But I do have many, many striped T-shirts.

My husband preferred T-shirts with goofy pictures and strange slogans and sayings. I especially remember two of his. One had a drawing of a big cow's head on it with the caption: "AMY THE ARMADILLO." The morose cow had a speech bubble over her head that said: "I am not an Armadillo." I could never understand what the cow had to do with the armadillo. Maybe he just wore the T-shirt to give people something to ponder. If you asked him to explain the meaning of the shirt, he would only give a secretive and cunning smile. His other favorite T-shirt simply said: "Beyond Repair." It was easier to understand but, for the wife of its wearer, harder to take. The statement seemed definitive somehow, but impossible to do anything about.

Some people subscribe to the idea that horizontal lines on one's clothing are fattening, while vertical lines are slimming. If I continue to eat so much chocolate I may need to move to wearing vertical striped shirts from the horizontal ones I prefer.

Marie Kondo is a Japanese woman who has known fame all over the world as an organizer and cleaning specialist for our homes. Her books have inspired many to get their lives in order, especially their wardrobes. She has inspired me. Among other things, she has propagated the idea for how to cleverly fold your clothes to store them in such a way that fits more of them into a drawer, while also allowing a better view of all your shirts.

In my wardrobe, the striped T-shirts fight for space. All of them are folded according to Marie Kondo's instructions, but if the drawer is full, it's full. In fact, I have two drawers of striped shirts. How did I collect so many striped shirts? A blue one with white stripes, a white one with red stripes, a yellow one with pink stripes, a green with white, and so on, and so on, and so on. My list of stripy shirt options is incredibly long and the combinations of stripes by colors sometimes seem endless when I open my organized drawers.

Perhaps I should will my stripy shirt collection to Jacob Dahlgren for his next work; perhaps he will be inspired. Perhaps I do have too many and should death clean those drawers.

But I remind myself that while stripes may not make you look young, they also do not make you look old and they always bring joy.

SURROUND YOURSELF WITH THE YOUNG(ER) OR *BUSVISSLA* TO YOUR YOUNGER SELF

When I left the launch party for my first book I was over-joyed. I was eighty-five years old and had just made my debut as an author. I asked my Swedish publisher, Abbe, how I was ever going to be able to thank him. He laughed and said:

"The only thing you need to do to thank me is this: always be kind to those younger than you."

Everyone is younger than me, so I have ample opportunity to practice this.

But it has been easy for me for other reasons. I've always had young people around me. Not just my five children, but also their kids and all the friends of my children and grand-children.

When I moved to Stockholm from Gothenburg in 2006, my husband had just passed away. I was devastated but at the same time curious to rediscover the big city I had lived in as a twenty-year-old art student. My husband and I had lived for many years in a tiny community on an island off the west coast of Sweden. Now I was going to visit galleries again.

Stockholm took me in. I found new friends. It was so much fun. A young man—Ulrik—wanted to do a blog with me about art. Young people, children of my old friends and of my own children, came to dinner. It was really different from the life I had lived on the island. A life I had also liked.

As you get older, it is important to listen to the young. It can be a lot more fun and interesting than listening to eighty-somethings shaking their fists, waving their canes, and saying everything was better in the old days.

My father was a doctor. He specialized in gynecology and obstetrics. In the doorway of the apartment house where we lived, there was a gold plaque with his name and profession. For some reason, it provoked a reaction in some of the boys who escorted me home after a dance or a party. I don't think the plaque would have caused the same reaction if Dad had a flower shop or built houses; those professions would hardly have led to blushing or giggles. To me their reaction to the plaque became a sort of measuring stick for how immature young teenage boys could be. Today I think their reactions were simply a bit comical.

When I was a little girl, maybe five, six years old, my father took me on his Sunday rounds in the hospitals to check on his patients. While he was doing his consultations, I had to wait in the hallway. I used that time to walk around and look at what hung on the walls or lay in the glass

cabinets. There were some strange instruments and pros-
thetics on display, and sometimes the kind nurses would
stop and talk to me for a while, so it never got to be boring.

As soon as Father was done, we would go to one, sometimes two art galleries to look at paintings, drawings, and
the occasional sculpture. I loved seeing everything and I
learned a lot of things I've used throughout my whole life.
Coming to another country, to a new city, and visiting an
art museum only to recognize a painting or an artist's work
I had seen a long time ago with my father always feels like
meeting an old friend.

Every now and then on Sundays—unless it rained,
which happens quite a lot in Gothenburg—we went down
to the harbor. My dad loved taking pictures, especially if it
was a bit foggy, as that acted almost like a soft filter for his
camera. I still have some of his harbor photos tucked away.
Sometimes, if he managed to steal a few slices of bread
without our housekeeper, Mrs. Karlsson, noticing, he would
bring a bag of them or maybe just bread crumbs tucked in
his pocket. Mrs. Karlsson was our housekeeper, but I think
she was really our boss—even Dad was a bit intimidated by
her. My father and I used to think that she sometimes kept a
little too strict an eye on our household's inventory. But we
didn't want to unnecessarily provoke her, so we had to be
careful.

It didn't take long before seagulls and terns were cir-
cling us, and ducks were swimming toward us. It was fun
throwing bread to them, trying to aim so that everyone got
a piece. When the bag was empty, Daddy would bring it to
his mouth, take a giant breath, inflate it, and then quickly

pop it. *Bang!!!* Away the birds flew, making a terrible racket as their wings flapped. It was Sunday's climax. Afterward, we went home to eat lunch.

My father was an "old-school" doctor. If he had promised a woman he'd be there when her children wanted out into the world, he kept his promise, even if it meant leaving the table in the middle of Christmas dinner. I remember him actually doing that one time, but he was soon home again. Happy as a lark.

As I was awaiting my fifth child, my parents came to visit. At the time we lived a couple of kilometers outside Gothenburg. My husband, Lars, wasn't home and I was nine months pregnant. The baby was fully baked. A nanny, who was supposed to take care of the older children while I was in the hospital, was already there. I made some coffee and gingerbread cookies and we sat down to have a chat. Suddenly my dad, who kept a close eye on everything, says, "I think you are in pre-labor; maybe we ought to go to the hospital." I hate sitting and waiting; pacing back and forth in the hospital hallway was something I had done a lot of and I always wanted to stay at home for as long as possible, but nevertheless we went.

But first I had to inform the nanny. I told her she was free to invite her boyfriend over if she wanted company. I had met him; he was no monster. She blushed and said, "He is already here. He climbed through my window last night."

"Ok," I said (keeping an open mind). "Very well. Make sure he enters through the front door from now on. Eat together and play family for a couple of days. You'll have a great time."

Dad followed me to the delivery floor but was not allowed into the delivery room. Hardly half an hour later the baby was born, but the medical staff soon became concerned as unfortunately the placenta hadn't fully come out. I began to become concerned too. The doctor asked if I had eaten something recently and I told him a ginger-bread cookie! He went on to pump my stomach. Damn that cookie! After that, I hardly ever have cookies.

The little girl, though, was a real beauty, so who cared about partially digested cookies in the end. She didn't have much hair, but she looked so pleased and made small, funny-sounding noises. Grandmother and grandfather came by again the next day to witness the miracle, and a telegram arrived from my husband on his way back from the USA. I was happy.

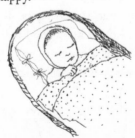

In speaking of happiness, I know what it is. Happiness is being surrounded by the young. My father knew it. I know it. And if you are over eighty, even a seventy-six-year-old is young. That, too, is happiness.

Of course, some people are idiots. Young or old. And I do not in any way want to say that young people are better than the old, or even more interesting or valuable. The thing with young people is that they lack experience, have new thoughts, have troubles and worries that most people my age have dealt with and gotten over. Surrounding yourself with young people is a way to stay in tune with the young person you yourself were at some point.

When I was young, I had great expectations: I was to become a world-famous painter. I would draw human longing; I would paint our souls. I would exhibit at the greatest galleries. Nothing would stop me.

When I hear young people talking about their dreams I am reminded of my young self, and also reminded that I am still the same person.

When I was young, there were three things I had always wanted to be able to do. They were: to play the trumpet, to tap-dance, and to *busvissla*—make the kind of extraloud whistle where you put your fingers in your mouth to amplify the sound. I don't know the English word. One of my daughters says it is close to a "wolf whistle," but not exactly—whatever it is, if you do it right, you can get anyone's attention.

I don't know why I have always wanted to do these

things. I think that some of the tasks are useful in unusual situations. Some are mostly just for the fun of it.

I knew a lady who was very elegant. One day we were out shopping in town. When we were ready, we wanted a cab to bring us home with our heavy packages. I could not believe my eyes, or my ears. The elegant lady did not wave her hand but emitted a clear and loud whistle—a *busvissla*. I was so impressed! Ever since I have tried to make that sound but without any result. I do not know why; maybe my lips, teeth, or tongue is not made for a *busvissel*.

To blow the trumpet is another way to make noise, but that was not the reason why I wanted to toot it myself. I really like trumpet music and loved to listen to Louis Armstrong, Bunny Berigan, and Harry James and others when I was young. I once borrowed a trumpet from a friend and tried to produce sounds from it. When my efforts did not produce any results at all, I gave it back. I told myself: to just listen is really much more enjoyable. And yet sometimes still I have the desire, the yearning, to make that noise.

Tap dance was popular in the thirties when I was born. My dad, who was a good dancer, could tap-dance. I never could, even when he tried to teach me as a small child. Tap-dancing was certainly a bit different from jitterbugging, which I did in Stockholm in the 1950s only twenty years later; jitterbugging I was able to do, maybe because I had a partner the same height in my beloved Lars.

Now I enjoy watching Fred Astaire and Ginger Rogers tap-dancing on YouTube and still have the desire to learn.

I have not yet given up. I think there is still hope. Maybe I will *busvissla* and tap-dance on my balcony one day. But I think I will spare my neighbors from trumpet blowing.

It is never too late to do anything, unless it really is too late and you are dead. The moment you start thinking it is too late, then you begin to die. I will keep going and do all I want to do. Maybe I'll have an art opening in New York. My father would have liked that.

APPENDIX: BONUS THOUGHTS AND TIPS ON DEATH CLEANING

HOW TO BROACH ONE OF LIFE'S MOST IMPORTANT TOPICS WITH YOUR LOVED ONES

As we age, many of us spend less time with our parents, and it can be hard to find a time to talk about death cleaning. During the holidays, many of us travel far and wide to reunite with brothers, sisters, and, above all, parents. Parents who, no matter how wonderful they are, are growing older. If you're unlucky, they are also the happy owners of a mountain of stuff, precious only to them. And guess who will have to eventually take care of all that stuff?

The holidays are that warm and lovely time of year when many of us consume more than we can handle. Presents, food, eggnog—it never stops. The days after the holidays are in fact a good time to talk about how much we consume in general, and about how many of us just have too much stuff. Maybe not on Christmas Eve per se, or your first visit home in a while—that would be a serious downer. But it is my experience that most families find the whole holiday experience exhausting, both financially and physically. This is something we can all relate to and talk about. Sit down and talk about the next holiday, whatever that holiday might be. In Sweden it is Midsummer. It might be Eid, Diwali, Purim; it could be a birth, wedding, adoption, funeral. The point is to talk.

Also, help your future self and make your parents truly happy: talk to them about what they want to do with all their stuff.

Writing my book on death cleaning helped my children and me talk about death in a constructive way. I have tried to make my approach fun and full of light. Talking and reading about difficult things always makes them easier. Death is a difficult topic, and we should really talk about it more.

Death is the toughest topic. Understandably. Death cleaning doesn't have to be: it's a very useful and practical approach to what can be a difficult or frightening topic. Whether you're middle-aged and facing your parents' passing, or thinking of your own, there is no moment better than the present to prepare for death. My goodness, we plan for everything. Why not death?

Death cleaning is not just for older people; I even think that people as young as forty can begin the process. If they continue regularly throughout their lives, they won't have so much to clean up when they are older and have less energy to do this demanding work.

For all the brave who start their own *döstädning*—I salute you! While you will make things easier for the people who come after you and life will be simpler for you, you will also discover that you have a good time doing it. It is a way to walk down your life's memory lane and see how the stories of your life weave together—as told through the things that you have kept—you will have a nice and thoughtful time.

When I was young, it was considered rude to speak your mind to an older person, including your own parents. Thankfully, today we generally believe that honesty is more important than politeness. At best, we combine the two. Talking about death cleaning can be a way for generations to talk to one another about what is important to them.

People often ask me how to approach the topic, how to even start the conversation. If your parents are getting old and you don't know how to bring up death cleaning, I would suggest paying them a visit, sitting them down, and asking the following questions in a gentle way:

"You have so many nice things; have you thought about what you want to do with it all later on?"

"Do you enjoy having all this stuff?"

"Could life be easier and less tiring if we got rid of some of this stuff that you have collected over the years?"

"Is there anything we slowly can do together so that you won't be overwhelmed later on by having to care for so much stuff?"

Old people often have balance issues. Rugs, stacks of books on the floor, and odd items lying about the house can be serious safety hazards. Perhaps this can be a way to start your discussion: Ask about the carpets. Are they really safe? Do they have to be there?

Perhaps this is where "tact" is still important, to ask these questions as gently and sensitively as you can. The first few times you bring up death cleaning, your parents may want to avoid the topic, or change the subject. If you are unable to get them to talk to you, give them a little time to think, then come back a few weeks or months later and ask again, perhaps with a slightly different angle.

Or ask them over the phone; mention that there are certain items in their house that you'd like to have and could you perhaps take them now? They might be relieved to get rid of a few things and finally see the promise and possible enjoyment of beginning to death clean for themselves. If you're too scared to appear "impolite" with your parents or startle them and you don't dare bring up death cleaning, then don't be surprised if you get stuck with it all later on!

Holiday time next year (or the year after, or year after). It's possible that your parents have passed away and you're going through the gifts you gave them last year. They really appreciated those gifts and held on to them. They also valued your conversation about their many possessions and started death cleaning. These lovely old people helped you all your life. Now they've helped you again. The attic is empty, the basement and garage too. They've given most of their stuff to charity, helping countless strangers in need, and some of the things you said you wanted they've kept and assigned to you with little notes. You loved these parents. You are sad that they are gone, but you do not miss all their stuff: you can cherish their memories, not cherish their *skräp* (Swedish for "junk")!

THE WORLD MAY ALWAYS BE ENDING, BUT SPRING CLEANING ALWAYS ARRIVES . . . UNTIL THE DAY IT DOESN'T

When spring is in the air, everything is lovely. Especially for those of us who live in countries with four seasons, it always feels as if it were years since we had a spring season.

We can hear birds chirping. They are not singing yet, but they will. We can see early spring flowers like winter aconite (*vintergäck*) and snowdrops popping up and the buds on trees are swelling.

Suddenly the sun seems to shine sharper than before and I realize that my windows are not as clean as I like them to be. Especially now that I've had my cataract operation, the streaks on my window are as shocking as the wrinkles I once saw in my mirror. The sun-highlighted streaks on my windows confirm for me that it is time for spring cleaning! Wow!

Maybe you have read about death cleaning? Maybe you have already started it. In that case, half of your work, perhaps even more, is already done, because you will have fewer things to dust and clean.

Anyway, I think there is something positive just in the word "spring-cleaning." Part of that is because you begin to remember the wonderful feeling when it is done. Spring will feel like it has arrived and your windows will sparkle, the world outside sunlight, bright and welcoming.

So let's get started:

1. Begin with the windows. With clean windowpanes it is easier to see the murkiest, forgotten areas inside your home.

2. Then go through clothes, fabrics like curtains, and smaller rugs. Air out, wash, or take out some items for dry cleaning. If you can dry your laundry outdoors, it will smell so fresh. And while you are at it, you may realize there were some things you never used during the winter months and which perhaps you can now get rid of. That will make next year's spring cleaning so much easier!

3. Dust and wipe all surfaces and shelves.

4. Vacuum-clean all soft furniture and pillows.

5. Vacuum-clean all floors and wash/mop them.

If you have a huge living space, you will need more than one day to get it all done, but for me today with my two-room apartment I can sit down and rest with a nice cup of tea or coffee and admire my work. Last, I will pick or buy some nice flowers and shout:

"Welcome, Spring!"

DEATH-CLEANING DISCOVERIES
IN THE TIME OF COVID
AND ANSWERS TO OTHER QUESTIONS
I HAVE RECEIVED FROM
CURIOUS NOVICE DEATH CLEANERS

You could be dead tomorrow. We all could—but should you really make others suffer because you were too lazy to sort your stuff, even during weeks or months of quarantine?

If you didn't death clean during the virus—what is your excuse?

1. PHOTOS: If you have too many photos, you can start by getting rid of those you regret that you ever took—be it because you no longer like the people in the picture, you look terrible, or you are covering the lens with your finger. After that, throw away all doubles. If you have thirty-four pictures from someone's party, wedding, or graduation, save three and send the rest to the person who was being celebrated or save the photos to give to them in person. It will brighten their day. Only save what your loved ones would like to look at.

2. KITCHEN CABINETS: Revisit your kitchen food cabinets now and then. Any food that has expired should be thrown out—but throwing out food is such a sad waste. Think about this when you shop. "Will I eat these lima beans? How about this extra-firm tofu? Or will it eventually end up being cleaned out?"

3. BOOKS: I still keep my favorite books on the book-shelf. I am rereading some that I had forgotten about and discovering I have a few new favorites, but the others I will pack up and give away maybe to charity, a secondhand bookstore, a library, a school, or a young person who loves to read.

4. LARGE FURNITURE: With all this done, you might have time to think about what is in the attic and garage—what can you get rid of—what to save, and please, have a look at your furniture. You probably wish to forget about all this, and you probably have, for twenty, thirty years. Now is the time to sort it out. Arm yourself with paper, pen, and Post-its and go to it. Thirty minutes a day is a good start. Work up to an hour a day. Reward yourself after every accomplish-ment: a nice coffee, a good cake, a warm shower or bath. If you hit three hours of death cleaning, I would suggest a cold beer.

5. TAKE NOTES: Have a notebook and pen in hand when you are going through your stuff. As you go through your belongings, you will get useful ideas. Of course, that little watercolor painting would be loved by an aunt or son. The binoculars would be perfect for Uncle Gustav, who is almost blind but still loves to go to the theater. With all the future gifts you find in your home, it will feel as if it were the night before Christmas. But if you do not write them down, you will forget your great gift ideas. You could even put a Post-it on each item with the recipient's name and a little thought about why this particular ceramic

piece feels perfect for one person, or that little rug to another and your porcelain cat to a third.

6. MAKEUP FROM THE SEVENTIES: When you have decided to get rid of the things you no longer need, it's not a good idea to just go dump it all in the garbage. Yes, it may be the easiest thing to do, the garbage is close by, but try to get rid of things in ways that also make you feel good about yourself and your tasks. Contact your municipality and ask how you should best deal with your stuff. Is there a recycling station? Or a place where you can leave the hazardous waste, i.e., leftover paint, broken glass, old makeup such as your frosted, shimmering light blue eye shadow, or shampoo from former centuries and anything else that is environmentally hazardous or that someone can injure themselves with?

7. PILLS: Go to the pharmacy with any pills or liquid medications that have been someone else's or your own, especially in cases where the expiration date has passed.

8. PERSONAL PAPERS: Unfortunately, as I write this, I do not think the pandemic has completely subsided. For the foreseeable future we should preferably not travel around unnecessarily and remain cautious about making new acquaintances. Instead it is a good opportunity to "visit" with old friends by going through all your old letters and even postcards that you saved. Enjoy your visits, but then run the letters and postcards through your shredder; it will

sound like music! If you do not have a shredder, scissors will do, or just rip stuff up with your hands as
you walk around your living space to provide a little
physical exercise. Perhaps all that physical activity
will help you sharpen your memory of the contents
and feelings in the letters without actually having to
keep them around to collect dust.

9. SENTIMENTAL ITEMS: Many people say they
want to get rid of things, particularly because of
space issues, and yet they keep them because of the
memories these items carry. And yet sometimes it
really is the right time to let something go. If you
have to get rid of an item you cherish, something
full of memories, take a picture of it. Then let the
thing go. You might say something to it as you part.
Nothing ceremonial or difficult. Make it easy, just say,
"Thank you, my dear."

All this will of course take time, and when you are finished with any remaining death cleaning, you can live happily for many years in your new uncluttered lifestyle. After
all, death cleaning is mostly about getting organized, not
dying.

In a way, I wish I hadn't been so efficient when I was first
thinking about and writing my first book, as I did a lot of
döstadning then. I now wish I had more death cleaning left
to do.

But there is a benefit. Now I can sit around thinking a
lot: What will happen next? Will we starve? Will there be a
war? Will there be a depression? A daughter says:

"One day at a time, Mom."

A son says:

"Do not regret; do not worry."

If we have done our death cleaning, we will know that our kids and our loved ones have a few nice things from us and can spend nice evenings in the park, instead of spending them sorting through my cupboards and closets.

Get started, MM.

April 2020

Adapted from a piece published on Psychologytoday.com

ACKNOWLEDGMENTS

A warm thank-you to everyone who has made this book possible: Susanna Lea, Nan Graham, Kara Watson, and Abbe Bonnier!

Also, a super thank-you to Stephen Morrison for cheering me on all the way and for an abundance of ideas. Also, my kids, well "kids," some of them are above sixty by now, but thank you for making my life deep and funny, and thanks to Jane and Lars for being right next door.

I THINK, THEREFORE I LAUGH

I THINK, THEREFORE I LAUGH

The Flip Side of Philosophy

JOHN ALLEN PAULOS

ALLEN LANE
THE PENGUIN PRESS

ALLEN LANE
THE PENGUIN PRESS

Published by the Penguin Group
Penguin Books Ltd, 27 Wrights Lane, London W8 5TZ, England
Penguin Putnam Inc., 375 Hudson Street, New York, New York 10014, USA
Penguin Books Australia Ltd, Ringwood, Victoria, Australia
Penguin Books Canada Ltd, 10 Alcorn Avenue, Toronto, Ontario, Canada M4V 3B2
Penguin Books India (P) Ltd, 11, Community Centre, Panchsheel Park, New Delhi – 110 017, India
Penguin Books (NZ) Ltd, Private Bag 102902, NSMC, Auckland, New Zealand
Penguin Books (South Africa) (Pty) Ltd, 5 Watkins Street, Denver Ext 4, Johannesburg 2094, South Africa

Penguin Books Ltd, Registered Offices: Harmondsworth, Middlesex, England

First published in the USA by Columbia University Press 2000
First published in Great Britain by Allen Lane The Penguin Press 2000

1

Copyright © John Allen Paulos, 2000

The moral right of the author has been asserted

Printed in England by Clays Ltd, St Ives plc

A CIP catalogue record for this book is available from the British Library

ISBN 0-713-99483-5

For my wife, Sheila

CONTENTS

PREFACE TO THE
SECOND EDITION

I Think, Therefore I Laugh is the second of my six books, and it has been out of print for a while. When Columbia University Press asked me if I would be interested in reissuing it and writing a new preface, I immediately agreed. With an author's myopic vanity, perhaps, I have always liked this little book, inspired, as it was, by Wittgenstein's quip that a book on philosophy might consist entirely of jokes. Since the book went out of print rather quickly, I've used it as a small quarry, and readers of my subsequent books may recognize bits and pieces of it in them. Moreover, many of the book's concerns are similar to those of my later books: misunderstandings of mathematics and science and of the relation between them, pseudoscience and its appeal, the uses and misuses of probability and statistics, humor and "higher-order" endeavors, the interplay between narrative and numbers.

Although my Ph.D. is in mathematics, specifically mathematical logic, I've always had an interest in analytic philosophy and its puzzles. It seemed to me when I wrote *I Think, Therefore I Laugh*, and it still seems, that the border between such philosophical abstractions and the concerns of everyday life is well worth exploring. The payoff to this exploration is of a largely intellectual sort. Recall one definition of a philosopher: he is the one who attends a conference on crime sentencing guidelines and delivers a paper on the meaning of "time" and the logical dilemma faced by imprisoned accomplices. Since social, economic, and topical issues are not the focus of this book (as they have been in a couple of my later works), there is no compelling temptation to update it. Aside from eliminating a number of infelicities and a few minor mistakes, I have not changed anything.

If I were to do the book over, I would choose a slightly different set of philosophical problems and a different set of jokes and parables and would develop them at a more leisurely pace. The presentation here is a bit relentless—something, something else, and then some other thing. Nevertheless, I reiterate and stand by the book's guiding insight: conceptual humor and analytic philosophy resonate at a very deep level. Did you hear what George Carlin and Groucho Marx said to Robert Nozick and Bertrand Russell? . . .

I THINK, THEREFORE I LAUGH

chapter one

TWO UNLIKELY PAIRS OF MEN

Ludwig Wittgenstein, the Austrian philosopher, once remarked that "a serious and good philosophical work could be written that would consist entirely of jokes" (Wittgenstein). If one understands the relevant philosophical point, one gets the joke. This has always seemed to me to be a wise remark, and this book is written in part to exemplify it. The book will contain a number of jokes as well as stories, parables, puzzles, and anecdotes, all of which in one way or another will relate to various philosophical problems. These stories and anecdotes will be linked by some (minimal) exposition and will be loosely integrated by topic. I hope they convey something of the flavor and substance of modern philosophy and dispel the feeling among some that philosophy is some sort of guide to life, a branch of theology or mathematics, or merely a matter of being stoical in the face of adversity.

One obvious criticism of an endeavor such as this is that for the philosophical points to be comprehensible, the jokes, examples, and metaphors relating to them must be placed in a relevant context and must be made part of a tightly reasoned argument. This is often true, of course, but for most of them the context and argument are at least partly implicit in the stories themselves. Consider, for example, the story of monkeys randomly typing on a typewriter and *King Lear* resulting. Even with no context or argument, the isolated story is thought-provoking, no matter that the "wrong" thoughts are often provoked. Similar remarks can be made about other classic stories—the sound of a tree falling in an uninhabited forest, Laplace's deterministic image of the universe as something like a giant and inexorable clock, or Plato's metaphor of the cave and the vague reflections of reality it allows. Often what one retains from a philosophical discussion are just such stories, vivid metaphors, examples, and counterexamples. The same thing holds for philosophical jokes.

Finally, even without much supporting context or argument, these stories and jokes are such that any fuller discussion or theory must accommodate and account for them. They provide part of the raw material that any reasonable philosophical theory must make sense of and thus should be part of the intellectual gear of all curious human beings.

Wittgenstein and Carroll

Let me consider a couple of unlikely pairs of men: the first, Wittgenstein and Lewis Carroll; the second, Bertrand Russell and Groucho Marx. The first pair I also compared in my previous book, *Mathematics and Humor*, from which this subsection is taken. However, in this book, among much else, I expand a bit on the comparison, as well as on a few other points made in *Mathematics and Humor*.

George Pitcher in "Wittgenstein, Nonsense, and Lewis Carroll" has written of some very striking similarities between the philosophical writings of Wittgenstein and the work of Carroll (Charles Lutwidge Dodson). Both men were concerned with nonsense, logical confusion, and language puzzles—although, as Pitcher notes, Wittgenstein was tortured by these things, whereas Carroll was, or at least appeared to be, delighted by them. (The relation between the two men is similar in this latter respect to that between Soren Kierkegaard and Woody Allen: same concerns, different approaches.) Pitcher cites many passages in *Alice's Adventures in Wonderland* and *Through the Looking Glass* as illustrating the type of joke Wittgenstein probably had in mind when he made the comment on philosophical jokes mentioned earlier.

The following excerpts are representative of the many in Lewis Carroll that concern topics that Wittgenstein also considered in his writings:

1. She [Alice] ate a little bit, and said anxiously to herself, "Which way? Which way?" holding her hand on the top of her head to feel which way it was growing, and she was quite surprised to find that she remained the same size. (*Alice in Wonderland*)

2. "That is not said right," said the Caterpillar. "Not *quite* right, I'm afraid," said Alice timidly; "some of the words have got altered."

"It is wrong from beginning to end," said the Caterpillar decidedly, and there was silence for some minutes. (*Alice in Wonderland*)

3. "Then you should say what you mean," the March Hare went on.

"I do," Alice hastily replied; "at least—at least I mean what I say—that's the same thing, you know."

"Not the same thing a bit!" said the Hatter. "Why, you might just as well say that 'I see what I eat' is the same thing as 'I eat what I see'!" (*Alice in Wonderland*)

4. "Would you—be good enough," Alice panted out, after running a little further, "to stop a minute just to get one's breath again?"

"I'm *good* enough," the King said, "only I'm not strong enough. You see, a minute goes by so fearfully quick. You might as well try to stop a Bandersnatch!" (*Through the Looking Glass*)

5. "It's very good jam," said the Queen.

"Well, I don't want any to-*day*, at any rate."

"You couldn't have it if you *did* want it," the Queen said. "The rule is jam to-morrow and jam yesterday—but never jam to-day."

"It *must* come sometimes to 'jam to-day,'" Alice objected.

"No, it can't," said the Queen. "It's jam every *other* day; today isn't any *other* day, you know."

"I don't understand you," said Alice. "It's dreadfully confusing." (*Through the Looking Glass*)

What do these examples have in common? They all betray some confusion about the logic of certain notions. One does not lay one's hand on top of one's head to see if one is growing taller or shorter (unless only one's neck is growing). One cannot recite a poem incorrectly "from beginning to end," since then one cannot be said to be even reciting that poem. (Wittgenstein was very concerned with criteria for establishing identity and similarity.) In the third quotation the Mad Hatter is presupposing the total independence of meaning and saying—an assumption that, Wittgenstein shows, leads to much misunderstanding. The next passage confuses the grammar of the word "minute" with that of a word like "train"; and the last illustrates that the word "to-day," despite some similarities, does not function as a date. Both these latter points were also discussed by Wittgenstein.

Wittgenstein explains that "when words in our ordinary language have prima facie analogous grammars we are inclined to try to interpret them analogously; i.e., we try to make the analogy hold throughout." In this way we "misunderstand . . . the grammar of our expressions and, like the fly in the fly bottle, sometimes need to be shown our way clear" (Wittgenstein). As I have mentioned, these linguistic misunderstandings can be sources of delight or of torture, depending on one's personality, mood, or intentions. Wittgenstein, for example, was tormented by the fact that a person does not talk about having a pain in his shoe, even though he may have a pain in his foot and his foot is in his shoe. Carroll, had he thought of it, probably would have written of shoes so full of pain that they had to be hospitalized.

Groucho Meets Russell

Just as Wittgenstein and Lewis Carroll shared some of the same preoccupations with language and nonsense, so Bertrand Russell and Groucho Marx were both concerned with the notion of self-reference. Furthermore, Russell's theoretical skepticism contrasts with Groucho's streetwise brand as do Russell's aristocratic anarchist tendencies with Groucho's more visceral anarchist feelings. I try to illustrate these points in the following dialogue between the two. Some of the topics mentioned in the dialogue will be discussed more fully in later chapters.

Groucho Marx and Bertrand Russell: What would the great comedian and the famous mathematician-philosopher, both in their own ways fascinated by the enigmas of self-reference, have said to each other had they met? Assume for the sake of absurdity that they are stuck together on the thirteenth metalevel of a building deep in the heart of Madhattan.

GROUCHO: This certainly is an arresting development. How are your sillygisms going to get us out of this predicament, Lord Russell? (*Under his breath:* Speaking to a Lord up here gives me the shakes. I think I'm in for some higher education.)

RUSSELL: There appears to be some problem with the electrical power. It has happened several times before and each time everything turned out quite all right. If scientific induction is any guide to the future, we shan't have long to wait.

GROUCHO: Induction, schminduction, not to mention horsefeathers.

RUSSELL: You have a good point there, Mr. Marx. As David Hume showed two hundred years ago, the only warrant for the use of the inductive principle of inference is the inductive principle itself, a clearly circular affair and not really very reassuring.

GROUCHO: Circular affairs are never reassuring. Did I ever tell you about my brother, sister-in-law, and George Fenniman?

RUSSELL: I don't believe you have, though I suspect you may not be referring to the same sort of circle.

GROUCHO: You're right, Lordie. I was talking more about a triangle, and not a cute triangle either. An obtuse, obscene one.

RUSSELL: Well, Mr. Marx, I know something about the latter as well. There was, you may recall, a considerable brouhaha made about my appointment to a chair at the City College of New York around 1940. They objected to my views on sex and free love.

GROUCHO: And for that they wanted to give you the chair?

RUSSELL: The authorities, bowing to intense pressure, withdrew their offer and I did not join the faculty.

GROUCHO: Well, don't worry about it. I certainly wouldn't

want to join any organization that would be willing to
have me as a member.

RUSSELL: That's a paradox.

GROUCHO: Yeah, Goldberg and Rubin, a pair o' docs up in
the Bronx.

RUSSELL: I meant my sets paradox.

GROUCHO: Oh, your sex pair o' docs. Masters and Johnson,
no doubt. It's odd a great philosopher like you having
problems like that.

RUSSELL: I was alluding to the set M of all sets that do not
contain themselves as members. If M is a member of
itself, it shouldn't be. If M isn't a member of itself, it
should be.

GROUCHO: Things are hard all over. Enough of this sleazy
talk though. (*Stops and listens.*) Hey, they're tapping a message on the girders. Some sort of a code, Bertie.

RUSSELL: (*Giggles*) Perhaps, Mr. Marx, we should term the
girder code a Godel code in honor of the eminent
Austrian logician Kurt Godel.

GROUCHO: Whatever. Be the first contestant to guess the
secret code and win $100.

RUSSELL: I shall try to translate it. (*He listens intently to the tapping.*) It says "This message is . . . This message is . . ."

GROUCHO: Hurry and unlox the Godels, Bertie boy, and st-
st-stop with the st-st-stuttering. The whole elevator shaft
is beginning to shake. Get me out of this ridiculous column.

RUSSELL: The tapping is causing the girders to resonate.
"This message is . . .

A LOUD EXPLOSION.

THE ELEVATOR OSCILLATES SPASMODICALLY
UP AND DOWN.

RUSSELL: ". . . is false. This message is false." The statement
as well as this elevator is ungrounded. If the message is
true, then by what it says it must be false. On the other
hand if it's false, then what it says must be true. I'm
afraid that the message has violated the logic barrier.

GROUCHO: Don't be afraid of that. I've been doing it all my
life. It makes for some ups and downs and vice versa, but
as my brother Harpo never tired of not saying: Why a
duck?

chapter two

LOGIC

Either—Or

There are no more basic principles of logic than the law of noncontradiction and the law of the excluded middle, and hence there is no better place to start the study of logic than with them. The law of noncontradiction states: "It is not the case that A and not A"—or, as Aristotle phrases it: "The same attribute cannot at the same time belong and not belong to the same subject and in the same respect." The law of the excluded middle states: "Either A or not A"—or, to state a specific instance of the law: "Either Wittgenstein was a redhead or he was not." (Symbolically, using $\sim$ for "not," $\wedge$ for "and," $\vee$ for "or," and parentheses ( ) to indicate that the statement within them is to be taken as a whole, the law of the excluded middle can be expressed as $A \vee \sim A$ and the law of noncontradiction as $\sim(A \wedge \sim A)$.)

Even such basic principles as these can cause problems, however, if they're used uncritically. Consider, for example, the law of the excluded middle. Below are three uses of the principle: one, unexceptionable and vaguely humorous; the second, puzzling and distinctly misleading; and the third, straightforward except to a minority.

The first is a story due to Leo Rosten (1968) that tells of a famous rabbi-logician who was so wise that he could analyze any situation no matter how complex. His students wondered, though, if his reasoning power could withstand a bout of drinking—so these respectful yet curious students induced him during a feast to drink enough wine to make him quite tipsy. When he fell asleep, they carried him to the cemetery and laid him on the ground behind a tombstone. They then hid themselves and awaited his analysis of the situation.

When he awoke they were most impressed by his Talmudic use of the law of the excluded middle: "Either I'm alive or I'm not. If I'm living, then what am I doing here? And if I'm dead, then why do I want to go to the bathroom?"

The second instance deals with future events. If it's true now that I shall do a certain thing next Tuesday, let's say fall off a horse, then no matter how I resist doing so, no matter what precautions I take, when Tuesday comes, I shall fall off a horse. On the other hand, if it's false now that next Tuesday I shall fall off a horse, then no matter what efforts I make to do so, no matter how recklessly I ride, I shall not fall off a horse that day. Yet that the prediction is either true or false is a necessary truth—the law of the excluded middle. It seems to follow that what shall happen next Tuesday is already fixed, that in fact not just one event next Tuesday but the entire future is somehow decided, logically preordained.

The problem with the above is not the law of the excluded middle, but the meaning, or rather meaninglessness, of statements of the form "It is true now that some specified event will happen."

Interestingly, a small minority of mathematicians deny that the law of the excluded middle is a law of logic. They object to statements such as "Either there is a string of eight consecutive 5s somewhere in the decimal expansion of π or there is not." Since there is lacking both a constructive proof of the existence of this string of 5s *and* a constructive proof of its nonexistence, the intuitionists and constructivists do not count the above third and most common use of the law of the excluded middle as being valid. For them, truth is a matter of constructive provability.

For quite different reasons, some quantum physicists also reject the applicability of the law of the excluded middle in some contexts. In fact ever since J. Lukasiewicz, an influential Polish logician of the 1920s, initiated the formal study of three-valued logics—true, false, undetermined (indeterminate, intermediate)—it has been an object of persistent, though limited, interest. In more benighted times, classical logicians who accepted the law of the excluded middle sometimes mocked those who did not with the following: "Did you hear the one about the Polish logician? He thought there were three truth values."

The moral of these stories is simply that even such a basic principle of logic can be misapplied, can be controversial. Logic is the most important theoretical tool we possess but, as with all tools, one must know how and when to use it. We want to avoid the sad fate of that proverbial tribe of Indians who, being experts on the theoretical properties of arrows (vectors), simultaneously fired arrows northward and westward whenever they spotted a bear to the northwest, or two arrows northward and one eastward when they spotted a bear north-northeast of them.

"If I had a horse, I'd horsewhip you!"

—Groucho Marx

Conditional statements can be tricky, even straightforward ones like the following.

*: "If George is hungry, then Martha is hungry." It's clear, I hope, that if * is true and George is hungry, then Martha is also hungry. It's equally clear that if George is hungry and Martha is not, then * is false. What if Martha is hungry and it's unknown whether or not George is? In almost all mathematical (and many logical) contexts, the convention is that in this case * is true. What if George is not hungry and it's unknown whether or not Martha is? Again, the convention most useful in mathematics and logic is that * is true.

To summarize: In mathematical, logical, and many everyday contexts any sentence having the form "If P, then Q" or "P implies Q," or, symbolically, "$P \rightarrow Q$," is (1) true whenever Q is true whether P is true or not, (2) true whenever P is false whether Q is true or not, and (3) false only when P is true and Q is false.

The following two stories are relevant and illustrative:

Bertrand Russell was discussing conditional statements of the above type and maintaining that a false statement implies anything and everything. A skeptical philosopher questioned him, "You mean that if 2 + 2 = 5, then you are the Pope?" Russell answered affirmatively and supplied the following amusing "proof":

"If we're assuming 2 + 2 = 5, then certainly you'll agree that subtracting 2 from each side of the equation gives us 2 = 3. Transposing, we have 3 = 2, and subtracting 1 from each side of the equation gives us 2 = 1. Thus since the Pope and I are two people and 2 = 1, then the Pope and I are one. Hence I'm the Pope."

LOGICIAN: So you see, class, anything follows from a false statement.

STUDENT: I'm afraid I'm lost.

LOGICIAN: It's really quite simple. Are you sure you don't understand?

STUDENT: All I'm sure of is that if I understood that stuff, then I'd be a monkey's uncle.

LOGICIAN: You're right there. (*Laughs*)

STUDENT: Why are you laughing?

LOGICIAN: You wouldn't understand.

STUDENT: Anyway, doc, if you're interested, we're having a party tonight.

LOGICIAN: And if I'm not interested?

STUDENT: What?

LOGICIAN: Thanks anyway, but I'm busy.

Nonmathematical contexts in which the foregoing analysis of if–then statements does not hold are not hard to find. Two statements that are false despite the falsity of their if–clauses are:

(1) If one were to place that nail in that glass of water, it would dissolve.

(2) If Harpo Marx had spoken in any of the Marx brothers' movies, World War II would have been averted.

The truth of such so-called subjunctive and counter-factual conditional statements does not, as in the case of mathematical conditional statements "If P, then Q," depend only on the truth or falsity of P and Q. Rather, it depends on the lawlike relationship that may or may not exist between P and Q.

Still, there are many uses of the mathematical conditional outside of logic and mathematics. If someone says "If it's raining, I'm going to punch you, and if it's not raining, I'm going to punch you," you can be sure that that person is using the mathematical conditional and that he intends to punch you.

Imagine a very rich superscientist who claims to have the power to predict with great accuracy which of two alternatives a person will choose. Imagine further that this scientist, let's call him Dr. Who, sets up a booth at a big World's Fair somewhere in the Midwest to demonstrate his abilities. Dr. Who explains that he tests people by using two boxes: box A is transparent and contains $1,000, whereas box B is opaque and contains either nothing or $1,000,000. Dr. Who tells each person that he or she can choose to take the contents of box B alone, or the contents of both box A and box B. However—and this is important—if, before the person chooses, Dr. Who believes that he or she will take the contents of both boxes, he leaves box B empty. On the other hand, if, before the person chooses, Dr. Who believes that he or she will take only the contents of box B, he places $1,000,000 in box B. Witnesses can verify afterward whether or not the $1,000,000 was placed in box B.

George and Martha are at the World's Fair and see for themselves that when a person chooses to take the contents of both boxes, 95 percent of the time box B is empty and the person gets to keep only the $1,000 in box A. They also note that when a person chooses to take the contents of box B alone, 95 percent of the time it contains $1,000,000, making the person an instant millionaire.

Now it's Martha's turn. Dr. Who examines her carefully, prepares the boxes, places them in front of her, and goes on to George. Impressed by these demonstrations, Martha chooses the contents of box B alone, hoping that Dr. Who accurately assessed her state of mind.

Next it's George's turn. Dr. Who examines him carefully, prepares the boxes, places them in front of him, and goes on to the next person. George reasons that since Dr. Who has already gone, and since the $1,000,000 either has or hasn't been placed in box B already, he may as well choose the contents of both boxes, thereby insuring himself at least $1,000 and possibly $1,001,000.

Finally it's your turn. Dr. Who has already examined you. What choice will you make? (Selling your right to make the choice to someone else for $500,000 is cheating.) The reaction to this paradox, due to the physicist William Newcombe and made well-known by the philosopher Robert Nozick, is intimately connected with one's attitude toward free will, determinism, and money.

Another, better-known story of choice and "higher powers" is due to Blaise Pascal, whose argument for becoming a Christian takes the form of a wager. If, according to Pascal (1966), one elects to believe in Christian doctrine, then if this doctrine is false, one loses nothing—whereas if it's true, one gains everlasting life in heaven. On the other hand, if one elects not to believe in Christian doctrine, then if this doctrine is false, one loses nothing—whereas if it's true, one suffers unrelenting punishment in hell. Only if one already believes in Christian doctrine, as Pascal did, does this argument have any persuasive power. The argument, of course, has nothing to do with Christianity, and could be used by any other religion (or cult) to rationalize other already-existing beliefs.

Everyone would agree that "*A* is false," "*B* is false," "*C* is false," and "One of *A, B,* or *C* is true" are, taken together, an inconsistent set of statements. Yet consider a lottery having 1,000,000 entrants, including you: you don't believe ticket 1 will win, nor ticket 2, nor ticket 3, . . . nor ticket 1,000,000; still, you do believe that *some* ticket will win.

A similar tale can be told about your attitude toward what you read in the newspaper. Unless you have first-hand knowledge of a story, you tend to believe each individual item you read in the paper; still, you also believe that some (many) of the items are false. An understanding of this seeming inconsistency is what prompts celebrities to sue sensationalist tabloids.

Get your tickets for the million-dollar lottery right here. Ten cents apiece, three for a quarter, five for a dollar. Step right up and win a million dollars—a dollar a year for a million years.

Sillygisms

People underestimate the extent to which play enters into any serious intellectual endeavor. Doing something for the what-if fun of it frees one from the shackles of goal-directed plodding and sometimes leads to otherwise unlikely new insights. (And if it doesn't, so what?) This tradition of intellectual play is very old. Even Plato was not above constructing silly "arguments" for his protagonists. A well-known example in the dialogue *Euthydemus* is the exchange between Dionysodorus and Ctessipus:

DIONYSODORUS: You say you have a dog?

CTESSIPUS: Yes, a villain of one.

DIONYSODORUS: And he has puppies.

CTESSIPUS: Yes, and they are very like himself.

DIONYSODORUS: And the dog is the father of them.

CTESSIPUS: Yes, I certainly saw him and the mother of the puppies come together.

DIONYSODORUS: And he is not yours.

CTESSIPUS: To be sure he is.

DIONYSODORUS: Then he is a father, and he is yours; ergo, he is your father, and the puppies are your brothers.

The argument seems silly, yet one with the same grammatical form seems unobjectionable: Fido is a dog. Fido is yours. Therefore Fido is your dog.

   An argument in a different vein is due to Raymond

Smullyan, who is some logician:

> Some cars rattle.
> My car really is some car.
> So no wonder my car rattles.

Getting back to dogs, why is one of the following arguments valid and the other not?

> A dog needs water to survive.
> Therefore my dog Linocera needs water to survive.

> A dog is barking in the backyard.
> Therefore my dog Ginger is barking in the backyard.

Perhaps surprisingly, the following two arguments are valid.

> Everybody loves a lover.
> George doesn't love himself.
> Therefore George doesn't love Martha.

Either everyone is a lover or some people are not lovers.

If everyone is a lover, Waldo certainly is a lover.

If everyone isn't, then there is at least one nonlover. Call her Myrtle.

Therefore if Myrtle is a lover, everyone is.

The validity of the first argument depends on two facts: (1) A person is a lover if that person loves anyone, himself included; (2) "If P, then Q" is true exactly when "If not Q, then not P" is. The validity of the second depends on the conditions under which "If P, then Q" is true.

36 inches = 1 yard
So 9 inches = $\frac{1}{4}$ yard
So $\sqrt{9}$ inches = $\sqrt{\frac{1}{4}}$ yard
Therefore 3 inches = $\frac{1}{2}$ yard

The temperature is 93.
The temperature will rise this afternoon.
Therefore 93 will rise this afternoon.

Most common manipulations of statements involving logical constants such as "all," "some," and "not" are intuitively clear. The negation of "Everyone is bald" (symbolically, $\forall x B(x)$—for all x, x is bald) is not "No one is bald" but rather "Someone is not bald" (symbolically, $\exists x \sim B(x)$—there exists an x such that x is not bald) or, more longwindedly, "It is not the case that everyone is bald."

Sometimes, though, the meanings of these constants are not so clear. "You can fool some of the people all the time" is, at second glance, ambiguous: it has two contrary interpretations. It can mean that there are certain gullible bumpkins, say George and Martha, who are bamboozled every day of the week; or it can mean that on any given day you choose, you'll always be able to fool some people—say, George on Monday, Martha and Waldo on Tuesday, Waldo and Myrtle on Wednesday, and so on. Using $P(x)$ for "x is a person," $T(y)$ for "y is a time," and $F(x,y)$ for "you can fool x at y," the first interpretation can be rendered symbolically as $\exists x \forall y \ (P(x) \wedge T(y) \rightarrow F(x,y))$, while the second is $\exists x \forall y \ (P(x) \wedge T(y) \rightarrow F(x,y))$.

An example of a less common logical word subject to similar ambiguities is the word "most":

*: "Most of the people there had read most of the books discussed."

Does * mean that more than half of the people there had read more than half of the books discussed, or does it mean that more than half of the books discussed had been read by more than half of the people there? That these interpretations differ can be seen if, for example, we assume that there were only three people there and only three books were discussed. The first interpretation corresponds to figure 1, and the second to figure 2.

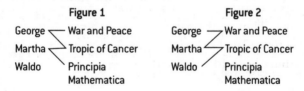

Figure 1	Figure 2
George — War and Peace	George — War and Peace
Martha — Tropic of Cancer	Martha — Tropic of Cancer
Waldo — Principia Mathematica	Waldo — Principia Mathematica

Even the simple logical word "is," maybe even *especially* the word "is," can be interpreted in everyday contexts in quite different ways. Consider the four statements below:

(1) George is Mr. Kyriacopoulos.

(2) George is anxious.

(3) Man is anxious.

(4) There is an anxious man here.

The first "is" is the "is" of identity: $g = k$. The second "is" is the "is" of predication: $A(g)$—g has the property A. The third "is" is the "is" of membership: $\forall x\,[M(x) \rightarrow A(x)]$. The fourth "is" is existential: $\exists x\, M(x)$.

It's odd that logical acuity, rather than helping one to clarify statements, often reveals hidden ambiguities within them. Instead of leading one to form more conclusions, it makes clear that fewer conclusions are justified. Bertrand Russell once observed (1956) that the keener one's sense of logical deduction, the less often one makes hard and fast inferences.

However, only for deductive inferences is this the case. Most "common sense" inferences do not depend on explicitly formulated knowledge or on any precise rules, but rather on a kind of tacit and natural process that is hard to describe. Thus mathematicians, accustomed as they are to clearly formulated principles and rigidly interpreted rules, sometimes have difficulty with "common sense" and often have a sense of humor characterized by the overly literal interpretation of terms and phrases.

⊚

MINISTER OF WAR: That's the last straw! I resign. I wash my hands of the whole business.
FIREFLY (GROUCHO): A good idea. You can wash your neck too.

⊚

GEORGE: In what two sports do face-offs occur?
WALDO: Ice hockey and . . . I give up. What's the other one?
GEORGE: Leper boxing.

⊚

No Parking signs often indicate "Violators will be towed," yet I've never yet seen a tow truck dragging anyone down the street. Trash cans that warn "Keep litter in its place" are also amusing if taken literally (litterly?): if something is litter, its place by definition, it would seem, is the ground.

⊚

Finally, consider this last sillygism, which leads into the topic of the next section:

This argument is helopita.
Nothing that's helopita is steedibeep.
Everything that's valid is steedibeep.
Therefore this argument is not valid.

Yet it is.

The Titl of This Section
Contains Three Erors

The study of self-referential statements dates back to Stoic logicians of the fourth and fifth century B.C. The oldest, best-known such paradox concerned Epimenides the Cretan, who stated: "All Cretans are liars." The crux of this so-called liar paradox is clearer if we simplify his statement to "I am lying" or, better yet, "This sentence is false." (Douglas Hofstadter writes of a more recent version, that of Nixonides the Cretin, who in 1974 stated: "This sentence is inoperative" [Hofstadter].)

Let us give the label Q to "This sentence is false." Now we notice that, if Q is true, then by what it says it must be false. On the other hand, if Q is false, then what it says is true, and Q must then be true. Hence, Q is true if and only if it's false.

The statement Q and variants of it are intimately connected with some of the deepest and most important ideas in logic and philosophy, and possibly even with consciousness itself. Despite this they are dismissed by most people as silly diversions, suitable only for amusing logicians and other useless people. I must admit that on Tuesdays I feel the same way, and since this is Tuesday, I will demonstrate how a relative of Q can be used to prove the existence of God. Consider the box below, which contains two sentences:

> 1. God exists.
> 2. Both of these sentences are false.

The second sentence is either true or false. If it's true, then both sentences are false. In particular, the second sentence is false; but the only way the second sentence can be false is for the first sentence to be true. Thus in this case God exists. On the other hand, if we assume directly that the second sentence is false, then again we must note that the only way for this to be is for the first sentence to be true. Thus in this case also God exists. Hence God exists.

Of course, in a similar way we can demonstrate that God had a hangnail, or that he doesn't exist, or that Ludwig Wittgenstein was in love with Mae West.

A related trick can be pulled with the following statement:

*: "If this statement is true, then God exists." If * is true, then it's true. On the other hand, if * is false, then the antecedent (the if clause) of * is false, which ensures that * itself is true. (Remember that a conditional if-then statement is true if the antecedent is false.) Thus in both cases * is true. Thus * is true, and hence the antecedent of * is true. Together these two facts ensure that the consequent (the then clause of *) is true. Hence God exists.

Even nonparadoxical statements can, if the situation is appropriate, be combined to yield a paradox. If Socrates were to say "What Plato just said is false," there would usually be nothing strange about the utterance. But if Plato were previously to have said "What Socrates says next is true," we would have a paradox.

There is an ancient story about the Sophist philosopher Protagoras, who agreed to instruct Euathlus in rhetoric so the latter could practice law. Euathlus in turn agreed to pay Protagoras his fee only after winning his first case. However, Euathlus chose not to practice law upon completing his training, and so Protagoras sued him for his fee. Protagoras maintained that he should be paid no matter what: he argued that if he won the case, he should be paid by order of the court; while if he lost, he should be paid by the terms of his agreement with Euathlus. Euathlus, who had learned something from his study with Protagoras, maintained that he should *not* pay no matter what: he argued that if he won the case, he should not pay by order of the court; while if he lost, he should not pay by the terms of his agreement with Protagoras.

Breakfast Scene

Big, brawny woman, hair in pincurls, wearing a torn bathrobe, to her scrawny, bald husband sitting in his underwear: "I want you to dominate me, to make me feel like a real woman."

As the last story might suggest, there is a close connection between these paradoxes and certain "double-bind" situations. The command "Be spontaneous" is another simple example, as is the injunction "Whatever you do, don't let the image of a sweet red watermelon covered with thick yellow mustard enter your mind." Unfortunately (or fortunately), most such situations that require contradictory behavior are more complex and somewhat more disguised—so disguised, in fact, that most people, especially those who consider self-referential paradoxes frivolous, do not realize that these situations pervade their lives. Situations, incidents, conversations are often so complexly textured that it's not uncommon for some aspect of these communications to "say" of itself that it's not true.

Consider the act of telling a joke. W. F. Fry and Gregory Bateson have shown that when someone tells a joke, there is usually some kind of behavioral cue—a different voice inflection, an arched eyebrow or wink, the use of a dialect, a mock serious tone, even the explicit clause, "Have you heard the one about. . . ." These cues, or metacues, qualify what is being said and function as a kind of nonverbal liar paradox. They say, in effect, "This whole business is false, unreal, not to be taken seriously; it's only joking." In fact, all dramatic performance—all art, even—has these two aspects: the content, and the frame or setting, which sets it apart from non-art and which says of itself, "This is not an everyday sort of communication. This is unreal."

A man, smiling and holding a small tree branch above his head, informs a bank teller, "This is a stick-up."

Russell's Dr. Goldberg and Dr. Rubin

Consider a country whose laws allow nonresident mayors—that is, some mayors live in the cities they govern, while others do not. A reform-minded dictator comes to power and orders that all the nonresident mayors, and only the nonresident mayors, live in one place—call it city C. City C now requires a mayor. Where shall the mayor of city C reside?

This story is a popularization of Russell's paradox, whose derivation is similar. We first note that some sets contain themselves as members. The set of all things mentioned on this page is mentioned on this page, and thus contains itself. Likewise, the set of all those sets with more than seven members itself contains more than seven members, and is thus a member of itself. Most naturally occurring sets do not contain themselves as members. The set of hairs on my head is not itself a hair on my head, and thus is not a member of itself. Similarly, the set of odd numbers is not itself an odd number, and thus does not contain itself as a member.

Dividing the set of all sets into two non-overlapping sets, let us denote by M the set of all those sets that do contain themselves as members, and by N the set of all those sets that do not contain themselves as members. In other words, for any set x, if x is a member of M, then x is a member of itself; and if x is a member of itself, then x is a member of

M. On the other hand, for any set *x*, if *x* is a member of *N*, then *x* is not a member of itself; and if *x* is not a member of itself, then *x* is a member of *N*.

Now we may ask whether *N* is a member of itself or not. (Compare this question with "Where does the mayor of city *C* live?") If *N* is a member of itself, then by definition of *N*, *N* is not a member of itself. But if *N* is not a member of itself, then by definition of *N*, *N* is a member of itself. Thus *N* is a member of itself if and only if it is not a member of itself. This contradiction constitutes Russell's paradox.

Robert Benchley once remarked: "There may be said to be two classes of people in the world: those who constantly divide the people of the world into two classes and those who do not." He should have added paradoxically that he belongs to the latter class.

Recall Groucho Marx's quip that he would never join any club that would be willing to have him as a member.

The following is a true story: A well-known philosopher was delivering a talk on linguistics and had just stated that the double negative construction has a positive meaning in some natural languages and a (very) negative meaning in others. He went on to observe, however, that in no language was it the case that a double positive construction has a negative meaning. To this, Sidney Morgenbesser, another well-known philosopher, who was sitting in the rear of the lecture room, responded with a jeering "Yeah, yeah."

V: "This sentence is true." *V* is a little odd, but not paradoxical. A variant of it, due to David Moser, reads: "This sentence is a !!! premature punctuator." "This sentence is graduellement changeant en français" is another.

Russell's resolution of the paradox is to restrict the notion of set to a well-defined collection of already-existing sets. In his famous theory of types, he classifed sets according to their type or level, thereby creating a set-theoretic hierarchy. On the lowest level, type 1, are individual objects. On the next level, type 2, are sets of type 1 objects. On the next level, type 3, are sets of type 1 or type 2 objects or sets; and so on. The elements of type n sets are sets of type $(n - 1)$ or lower. In this way Russell's paradox is avoided, since a set can be a member only of a set of a higher type and not of itself. Informal uses of this idea are commonplace: characters in cartoons, television, and movies are forever saying things like they're anxious about their anxieties, bored with their boredom, or tired of being tired.

The liar paradox can be avoided in a similar way. Applying a hierarchical solution to Epimenides' utterance requires that "All Cretans are liars" be assigned a higher type than other statements made by Cretans. We make a distinction between type I statements (usually called first-order statements), which do not refer to other statements; second-order statements, which refer to first-order statements; third-order statements, which refer to first- and second-order statements; and so on. Thus if Epimenides the Cretan states that all statements made by him are false, he is to be understood as making a statement that does not apply to itself; he is making a statement of an order higher than that of his other statements. In this way the self-negation of the liar paradox is prevented.

The following three statements are first-, second-, and third-order statements, respectively:

(1) Wittgenstein was bald.

(2) Statement (1) is false.

(3) Statement (2) is true.

This hierarchical notion of truth for statements has been extensively developed by the logician Alfred Tarski and others. It is not, however, the only way to handle these questions. An alternative approach, due to the philosopher Saul Kripke, takes statements like Q—"This sentence is false"—to be "ungrounded," there being no ground, no first-order statement, from which to build up to the truth or falsity of *Q*. Statements in the Kripke formulation are not (as in the Tarski account) assigned fixed levels or orders, but attain their level naturally depending on what other statements have been made and the facts of the situation. (Cf. the Plato-Socrates story above.) The truth or falsity of these statements is determined in a gradual, inductive manner, with not every sentence receiving a truth value (e.g., *Q*). Self-referential statements are allowed, though, and can, under appropriate circumstances, receive a truth value.

A literal interpretation of "self-addressed stamped envelope" is a stamped envelope addressed to itself. Ideal for instant delivery.

"You always overreact. You never ever respond moderately. If you shrug one more time, I'm going to scream."

DYSLEXIA

Language and Metalanguage: Do You Get It?

Implicit in the discussion of language levels in Russell's theory of types is a very general and extremely important distinction in logic and philosophy, that between object language and metalanguage. Object-level statements are statements within a (usually) formal system that is the object of study. Examples are:

(1) $A \wedge B \rightarrow \sim C \vee B$

   (If A and B, then either not C or B)

(2) $\forall x \exists y P(x, y)$

   (For all x there is a y such that x bears relation P to y)

(3) $p | (x^2 - 1) \rightarrow p | x$

   (If p divides $x^2 - 1$, then p divides x)

Metalevel statements are statements about the formal system, or about the object-level statements within it. Examples are:

(1) Statement Q has two different interpretations.

(2) Statement S is true but not provable.

(3) P, S, and Q are inconsistent.

If one is studying Japanese grammar, Japanese is the object language and English is the metalanguage.

Groucho says to an acquaintance, "Did you hear the one about the organization for people whose IQs are in the bottom 2 percent? I was just looking at its newsletter called DENSA." Groucho stops, bends closer, and says casually, "Do you get it? Do you get it?" The acquaintance, thinking he's being asked if he understands the joke, answers "Yes," to which Groucho rejoins, "I'm surprised. I thought you were a little brighter than that."

Risking a charge of pedantry, I'll note that Groucho's acquaintance misinterprets "Do you get it?" as a metalevel question about the joke, and not an object-level question that is part of the joke.

The tortoise in Lewis Carroll's "What the Tortoise Said to Achilles" (excerpted below) makes the opposite mistake. He confuses the metalevel rule C with the object-level statements A, B, and Z. C needs no further rule to explain when and how it applies, yet the tortoise insists on a meta-metalevel rule D to do just that, and then a meta-metametalevel rule E to explain when and how D applies, and so on. The tortoise just isn't playing the logic game.

"That beautiful First Proposition by Euclid!" the Tortoise murmured dreamily. "You admire Euclid?"

"Passionately! So far, at least, as one can admire a treatise that won't be published for some centuries to come!"

Well, now, let's take a little bit of the argument in that First Proposition—just two steps, and the conclusion drawn from them. Kindly enter them in your note-book. And in order to refer to them conveniently, let's call them *A*, *B*, and *Z*:

A) Things that are equal to the same are equal to each other.

B) The two sides of this Triangle are things that are equal to the same.

Z) The two sides of this Triangle are equal to each other. . . .

"I'm to force you to accept *Z*, am I?" Achilles said musingly. "And your present position is that you accept *A* and *B*, but you *don't* accept the Hypothetical—"

"Let's call it *C*," said the Tortoise.

"—but you *don't* accept C) If *A* and *B* are true, *Z* must be true."

"That is my present position," said the Tortoise.

"Then I must ask you to accept *C*."

"I'll do so," said the Tortoise, "as soon as you've entered it in that note-book of yours. What else have you got in it?"

"Only a few memoranda," said Achilles, nervously fluttering the leaves: "A few memoranda of—of the battles in which I have distinguished myself!"

"Plenty of blank leaves, I see!" the Tortoise cheerily remarked. "We shall need them *all*!" (Achilles shuddered.) "Now write as I dictate:—

A) Things that are equal to the same are equal to each other.

B) The two sides of this Triangle are things that are equal to the same.

C) If A and B are true, Z must be true.

Z) The two sides of this Triangle are equal to each other."

"You should call it D, not Z," said Achilles. "It comes *next* to the other three. If you accept A and B and C, you *must* accept Z."

"And why *must* I?"

"Because it follows *logically* from them. If A and B and C are true, Z *must* be true. You don't dispute *that*, I imagine?"

"If A and B and C are true, Z *must* be true," the Tortoise thoughtfully repeated. "That's *another* Hypothetical, isn't it? And, if I failed to see its truth, I might accept A and B and C, and *still* not accept Z, mightn't I?"

"You might," the candid hero admitted; "though such obtuseness would certainly be phenomenal. Still, the event is *possible*. So I must ask you to grant *one* more Hypothetical."

"Very good. I'm quite willing to grant it, as soon as you've written it down. We will call it D) If A and B and C are true, Z *must* be true. Have you entered that in your note-book?"

"I *have*!" Achilles joyfully exclaimed, as he ran the pencil into its sheath. "And at last we've got to the end of this ideal racecourse! Now that you accept *A* and *B* and *C* and *D*, *of course* you accept ζ."

"Do I?" said the Tortoise innocently. "Let's make that quite clear. I accept *A* and *B* and *C* and *D*. Suppose I *still* refused to accept ζ?"

"Then Logic would take you by the throat, and *force* you to do it!" Achilles triumphantly replied. "Logic would tell you 'You can't help yourself. Now that you've accepted *A* and *B* and *C* and *D*, you must accept ζ!' So you've no choice, you see."

"Whatever *Logic* is good enough to tell me is worth *writing down*," said the Tortoise. "So enter it in your book, please. We will call it E) If *A* and *B* and *C* and *D* are true, ζ must be true. Until I've granted *that*, of course I needn't grant ζ. So it's quite a *necessary* step, you see?"

"I see," said Achilles; and there was a touch of sadness in his tone.   *(Carroll)*

Godel's famous incompleteness (meta)theorem also depends crucially on the object-metalevel distinction. Godel considered a simple formal system containing the basic axioms of the arithmetic of whole numbers. He methodically assigned each object-level statement a unique code number; he also assigned a code number to each proof of an object-level statement. By means of this coding, object-level statements about numbers can also be understood as expressing metalevel statements about the system, or about individual object-level statements. If one is careful and clever, one can find a statement *G* that is true if and only if it is unprovable.

Loosely speaking, we note that this object-level statement about whole numbers says of itself, via the numerical coding, that it is not provable. If the axioms are all true and the system is consistent, it is possible to conclude that such a statement *G* (about whole numbers, remember) is neither provable nor disprovable from the axioms—that it is independent of them. The same idea can be extended to show that any formal system is incapable of proving some truths and thus that no formal system can prove all truths.

The following old joke has something of the same flavor: A new prisoner was puzzled because his fellow inmates laughed whenever one of them called out a number. He was told that the numbers were a code for certain jokes, which thus did not need to be repeated verbatim. Intrigued, the new prisoner called out "63" and was greeted by total silence. Later his cellmate explained that everything depends on how the joke is told.

This metajoke can, I suppose, itself be assigned a code number and. . . .

Comedians, after a joke has failed, often follow it with a self-deprecating comment on the joke, thereby salvaging at least a metajoke. So do authors.

This sentence has three erors. As in the titl of a previous section, one of these erors is of a quite different type (level) than the other two.

Related to the language-metalanguage distinction—in fact, a special case of it—is the use-mention distinction. To illustrate, the first pair of sentences below uses the words "laughing" and "Daniel," while the second pair merely mentions them:

(1) Leah was laughing at the Smurf cartoons.

(2) Daniel loves lawnmowers.

(1') "Laughing" contains eight letters.

(2') "Daniel" is a boy's name.

That the distinction can be grasped by a five-year-old is demonstrated by the following true story: A colleague of mine, working on a paper at home in his study, was disturbed repeatedly by his five-year-old son's use of the expletive "shit" in the next room whenever his blocks collapsed. My colleague firmly warned him not to use the word anymore. Returning to his study he heard his son say it again, whereupon he whirled around and barged into his son's room only to hear him continue defensively ". . . is a bad word. 'Shit' is a bad word. Right, Daddy?"

Failure to distinguish between using and mentioning can also lead to arguments like the following concerning former-President and Mrs. Ford:

Betty loves Ford.
Ford is a four-letter word.
Therefore Betty loves a four-letter word.

i should begin with a capital letter.

Meaning, Reference, and Dora Black's First Husband

Meaning, reference, names, and descriptions: these notions are at the heart of many disputes in philosophical logic. Whatever the resolution of these, some well-known puzzles will have to be solved (or dissolved).

The meaning of "meaning" is difficult if not impossible to formulate in full generality. One clear though wrongheadedly narrow account was provided by the early logical positivists, who identified the meaning of a proposition with its method of verification—that is, with whatever observations point to its truth. Using this so-called verifiability principle, they thought they had managed to do away with metaphysics, theology, and ethics, whose propositions are seemingly unverifiable. Hence we have the boring sterility of the logical positivists' program. One major problem with this theory of meaning, of course, is that the verifiability principle itself is embarrassingly not verifiable. "Reference" too is a difficult notion to pin down. Still, whatever these terms mean we can say something about the connection between them.

Two terms or expressions can refer to the same entity (or set of entities) though they differ in meaning. To use a classical example, due to the logician Gottlob Frege, we note that "the morning star" and "the evening star" certainly differ in meaning, or, as is sometimes said, in intension (with an *s*). It required an empirical discovery to realize that both those expressions have the same referent (i.e., both refer to the same entity)—the planet Venus. Similarly, "the younger coauthor of *Principia Mathematica*" and the "first husband of Dora Black," though they do not mean the same thing, both refer to Bertrand Russell. The term "renates" means "animals with kidneys," while "cordates" means "animals with hearts"; yet they both refer to the same collection of animals, since it so happens that all animals with hearts have kidneys and vice versa.

A term or expression is said to occur *extensionally* in a sentence if replacing it with any other term or expression with the same referent does not change the truth or falsity of the sentence. In many contexts, certainly in all purely mathematical ones, this substituting of equals for equals is extensional and causes no problem. Its use in fact was so obvious to Euclid that he included it in his development of plane geometry as "a common notion" not in need of any further elucidation or proof. If a is greater than x^2 <ms> 1, and $a = b$, then b is greater than x^2 <ms> 1. Still, outside of mathematics this substitution principle can fail—as the following arguments show:

The president thought that the city of Copenhagen was in Norway.

The city of Copenhagen is the capital of Denmark.

Therefore the president thought the capital of Denmark was in Norway.

It is a mathematical theorem that the number six is greater than the number three.

The number six is the number of men who were husbands of Elizabeth Taylor.

Therefore it is a mathematical theorem that the number of men who were husbands of Elizabeth Taylor is greater than the number three.

Statements or expressions can have a meaning yet lack a referent (at least according to many philosophers' accounts). Russell's celebrated "The present King of France is bald" is an example. Russell takes it to mean "There is a single person who is King of France, and that person is bald"; on this analysis it is meaningful but false.

GEORGE: Peter Pan doesn't exist.

MARTHA: You mean the boy who flies through the air, who does battle with Captain Hook, and whom little children love.

GEORGE: Yes, he doesn't exist.

MARTHA: Who doesn't exist?

GEORGE: Peter Pan.

WALDO: When are you going to pay the balance of this bill, George?

GEORGE: Don't worry. I'll get it to you by the second Tuesday of next week.

Sometimes even more serious difficulties can arise, as when George announces, "My brother is an only child."

Just as two terms can differ in meaning yet have the same referent, a term can have many referents but only one meaning. "My father," for example, when uttered by me refers to my father, whereas when uttered by Waldo, it refers to Waldo's father (surprise). Similarly, words like "you" or "I," "yesterday" or "tomorrow," "here" or "there" refer to different entities depending on when, where, and by whom they're uttered.

A man and an acquaintance of his are walking down a street one afternoon. The man spots his wife and his mistress talking in a café and amusedly remarks, "Imagine a mistress spending the morning with her lover and then having a friendly chat with his wife that afternoon." The acquaintance, a pale, shocked look on his face, responds "How did you find out?"

Two clergymen were discussing the present sad state of sexual morality. "I didn't sleep with my wife before we were married," one clergyman stated self-righteously. "Did you?"

"I'm not sure," said the other. "What was her maiden name?"

Analytic vs. Synthetic, Boole vs. Boyle, and Mathematics vs. Cookery

An analytic truth is one that is true in virtue of the meanings of the words it contains, and a synthetic truth is one that is true in virtue of the way the world is. ("If George is smelly and bald, then he's bald," vs. "If George is smelly, then he's bald." "Bachelors are unmarried men," vs. "Bachelors are lascivious men." "UFOs are flying objects that have not been identified," vs. "UFOs contain little green men.") This distinction is a sprucing up of Immanuel Kant's original one, which in turn derives from similar distinctions due to David Hume and Gottfried Leibniz. Some philosophers, in particular the American W. V. O. Quine, have argued that the distinction is not hard and clear, but rather one of degree or convenience. It is still, even if not absolute and immutable, a useful distinction.

When Molière's pompous doctor announces that the sleeping potion is effective because of its dormitive virtue, he is making an empty, analytic statement, not a factual, synthetic one. The same thing can be said about the White Knight in *Through the Looking Glass* when he describes to Alice the song he wants to sing:

"It's long," said the Knight, "but it's very, *very* beautiful. Everybody that hears me sing it—either it brings tears to their eyes, or else—"

"Or else what?" said Alice, for the Knight had
made a sudden pause.

"Or else it doesn't, you know."

Likewise, "A well-told joke will not be funny unless it's
well-told," despite the appearance that it's saying something
substantial, is simply an analytic truth. It is equivalent to "If
a well-told joke is funny, it is well-told."

Conversely, synthetic truths are sometimes mistaken
for statements that are analytically true or analytically false.
Examples are "The second-place Chicago White Sox took
the field wearing white sox," or the perennial "The Holy
Roman Empire was not holy, Roman, or imperial." Some
of the pronouncements on space and time in Einstein's
theory of relativity are also seen now to be synthetic truths
and not, as they appeared and still appear to many people,
analytic falsehoods.

Even more common are exchanges like the following,
in which prejudices are preserved by making them, through
redefinition, analytically true:

GEORGE: Scotsmen don't buy jewelry.

MARTHA: But MacGregor just bought fourteen diamond
    necklaces.

GEORGE: MacGregor is not a true Scotsman, then.

Capitalists (neurotics, Jews, Englishmen, Greeks, blacks,
etc.) don't do such and such. But so and so did do such and
such. Well then, he's not a real capitalist (neurotic, Jew,
Englishman, Greek, black, etc.).

It can be said that the difference between analytic truths
and synthetic truths is the difference between an "*o*" and a

"*y*," between Boole's laws of logic and Boyle's laws of gases. It is roughly the difference between the formal sciences (mathematics, logic, and linguistics) and the empirical sciences (physics, psychology, and cooking).

Bertrand Russell once wrote:

> Pure mathematics consists entirely of such asservations as that, if such and such a proposition is true of *anything*, then such and such another proposition is true of that thing. It is essential not to discuss whether the first proposition is really true, and not to mention what the anything is of which it is supposed to be true. . . . If our hypothesis is about *anything* and not about some one or more particular things, then our deductions constitute mathematics. Thus mathematics may be defined as the subject in which we never know what we are talking about, nor whether what we are saying is true.   *(Russell)*

Though the ubiquity of people who do not know what they're talking about nor whether what they're saying is true may suggest that mathematical talent is widespread, the quote does give a succinct summary of the formal approach to mathematics. Certain axioms, expressed in a formal language, are laid down; precise rules of inference are formulated; and theorems are derived from the axioms by means of the rules of inference. What anything means is (or can be) ignored. In this respect, mathematics can be compared to the game of chess—the axioms to the initial positions, the rules of inference to the rules governing the allowable moves, and theorems to subsequent positions of the pieces. Mathematical truths, in particular Euclidean geometric truths, were thought to be (using Immanuel Kant's terms) synthetic a priori—that is, they were considered to be true because of the way the world is, yet independent of experience. The development of consistent non-Euclidean geometries by Bolyai, Lobachevsky, and Gauss led to the realization, implicit in Russell's quote, that points, lines, and other primitive geometric terms and relations could be taken to be *anything at all* that satisfied the formal axioms containing these terms and relations, and that geometrical theorems were simply any formal statements that followed from the axioms by means of the rules of inference.

Not until (if ever) the terms are given a particular empirical meaning do the notions of truth or falsity become appropriate. As the French mathematician Poincaré once wrote, "What are we to think of the question: Is Euclidean geometry true? It has no meaning. . . . One geometry cannot be more true than another; it can only be more convenient" (Poincaré 1913). This is because mathematics chases not truth (a metalevel notion) but formal consequences (provability, an object-level notion), not "Is this true of the world?" but "Does this follow from that?" Einstein phrased it: "As far as the properties of mathematics refer to reality, they are not certain: and as far as they are certain, they do not refer to reality" (Einstein). Mathematical truths, by and large, are certain because they are analytic; physical truths are not certain because they are synthetic.

George goes to the You-Bet-Your-Life computer dating service to register his requirements (axioms). He wants someone who is white, not very talkative, comfortable in fur, yet disdainful of city life. The computer sends him a polar bear.

Immanuel Kant goes to the Lobachevsky Lumber Company to order a flat board with which to cover his desk. Feeling mischievous, he asks for a surface that satisfies the (first four) axioms of Euclidean plane geometry. The lumber company gives him a saddle-shaped piece of wood.

That *synthetic* scientific laws and facts cannot be determined a priori now seems a commonplace. That this was not always the case is illustrated by the following excerpt from Francesco Sizi wherein he "argues" that, contrary to what his contemporary Galileo had seen through his telescope, Jupiter could have no satellites:

> There are seven windows in the head, two nostrils, two ears, two eyes and a mouth; so in the heavens there are two favorable stars, two unpropitious, two luminaries, and Mercury alone undecided and indifferent. From which and many other similar phenomena of nature such as the seven metals, etc., which it were tedious to enumerate, we gather that

the number of planets is necessarily seven. . . .
Moreover, the satellites are invisible to the naked eye
and therefore can have no influence on the earth
and therefore would be useless and therefore do not
exist.

The German philosopher Hegel, just before the discovery of the asteroid Ceres, also chastised astronomers for
not paying more attention to philosophy—a science that
would, according to Herr Hegel, have shown them that
there could not possibly be more than seven planets.

I'd like to close this chapter with a short collection of logical jokes and stories. The first "joke" consists merely of pairs of phrases, each element of the pair sharing the same grammar yet having a different logic (in a broad, informal sense of "logic"):

"Waldo likes to move his rooks out early," vs. "The MATE-IAC II computer likes to move its rooks out early."

"Going on to infinity," vs. "going on to Paris."

"Honesty compels me," vs. "The IRS compels me."

"The present Czar of Russia is obese," vs. "The present president of the United States is obese."

"Being a baseball player," vs. "being a baseball."

"An alleged murderer," vs. "a vicious murderer."

"Have you stopped beating your husband?" vs. "Have you voted for Megalomeeti yet?"

"If only Pat had a different job," vs. "If only Pat had a different sex."

"Before the world began," vs. "before the Phillies game began."

"Studying for a physics test," vs. "studying for a urine test."

Modern analytic philosophy has sometimes been called linguistic therapy, and philosophers like Wittgenstein, Ryle, and Austin have devoted much effort and analysis to curing some of the "linguistic diseases" lurking all over, in particular in phrases such as the above.

T.V. SPORTSCASTER: Folks, we're running out of time so I'll have to hurry with the baseball scores. 4 to 2, 6 to 3, 8 to 5, and in a real cliff-hanger, 2 to 1.

T.V. FOOTBALL COMMENTATOR: These teams really came to play today.

PEASANT: Is kebab with an "a" or an "o"?
SUFI MASTER: With meat.

10-YEAR-OLD: Pete and Repeat were walking down the street. Pete fell down. Who was left?
7-YEAR-OLD: Repeat.
10-YEAR-OLD: Pete and Repeat were walking down the street. Pete fell down. Who was left?

MARTHA: George, in this game cheating is allowed.

A wife laughs at her distraught husband who has a loaded revolver at his temple. "Don't laugh," he tells her. "You're next."

Title of Book: *20 Ways to Regain Your Virginity*

There was once a very brilliant horse who mastered arithmetic, algebra, plane geometry, and trigonometry. When presented with problems in analytic geometry, however, the horse would kick, neigh, and struggle desperately. One just couldn't put Descartes before the horse.

What's a question that contains the word "cantaloupe" for no apparent reason?

COSTELLO: Who's on first?
ABBOT: Yeah. Who is on first, Johnson's on second.
COSTELLO: Who's on first?

ABBOT: Right, Who is. Johnson's on second and Walters is up to bat.

COSTELLO: But who is on first?

WAITER: Would you like white wine or red wine with your dinner?

GEORGE: It doesn't matter. I'm color blind.

Speaking of liquids, the following is an old conundrum: A tablespoon of water is removed from an 8-oz. glass of water, placed in an 8-oz. glass of wine, and the resulting mixture stirred. A tablespoon of the mixture is then removed, placed in the water glass, and stirred. Is there more wine in the water or more water in the wine?

If you're sick of such logical niceties, the last story may please you. Bertrand Russell, in satirizing the empty precision of some philosophers, told of a man who comes to a fork in the road. He asks a philosopher who happens to be loitering there, "Which way to the town of Dresher?" The philosopher responds, "Which one of these two roads here?"

"Yes, yes."

"It's the town of Dresher you're looking for?"

"Yes, yes."

"You want to follow one of these two roads here to the town of Dresher?"

Growing impatient, the man repeats, "Yes, which road leads to Dresher?"

"I don't know."

The philosopher was not a very good one. He should have asked the man if he was sure that one and only one of the two roads really did lead to Dresher, before telling him that he didn't know which. A more significant and disturbing revelation of ignorance begins the next chapter.

chapter three

SCIENCE

Induction, Causality, and Hume's Eggs

WOMAN: Doctor, doctor. You must help me. My husband thinks he's a chicken.

DOCTOR: That's terrible. How long has he thought this way?

WOMAN: As long as I can remember.

DOCTOR: Then why didn't you see me sooner?

WOMAN: I would have, but we needed the eggs.

If the doctor were to answer that he too needed the eggs, we would have something analogous to the problem of induction:

WOMAN: Professor, professor. You must help me. My husband uses an inductive argument to justify the use of inductive arguments.

PROFESSOR HUME: That's terrible. How long has he acted this way?

WOMAN: As long as I can remember.

HUME: Then why didn't you see me sooner?

WOMAN: I would have, but we needed (the conclusions of) the inductive arguments.

HUME: I'm afraid I need them too.

Let me summarize what is usually referred to as Hume's traditional problem of induction or, as Russell once called it, "the scandal of philosophy." We, every day of our lives, confidently use inductive arguments (arguments whose conclusions go beyond, contain more information than, the premises). Why are we so confident that these arguments usually yield true conclusions from true premises? There certainly is no deductive argument that since the sun has risen regularly in the past, it will probably rise tomorrow, or that since stones that have been dropped have always fallen in the past, they will probably fall when dropped in the future. It seems that the only argument for the continuation of these regularities is an inductive one: since these regularities have obtained in the past, they will probably continue into the future. But to try to justify the use of inductive arguments by an inductive argument is clearly circular and begs the question. To put the matter a little crudely, the answer to the question "Why will the future be like the past in certain relevant respects?" is nothing more satisfying than "It will be because past futures have been like past pasts in certain relevant respects." This is helpful only if the future will be like the past—which is the point at issue.

There have been many attempts to clean up "the scandal of philosophy." One way out is just to accept a nonempirical principle of the uniformity (over time) of nature. The problem with this "solution" is that it also begs the question; it is equivalent to what is to be established. It has the advantage, as Russell said in a different context, of "theft over honest toil." Another attempted way out is to note that some inductive arguments are of higher order than others, and to try to make use of this hierarchy (of inductive arguments, meta-inductive arguments, meta-metainductive arguments, and so on) to somehow justify induction. This does not quite work—or rather it works too well, and "justifies" a lot of weird practices.

Charles Saunders Peirce and Hans Reichenbach have advanced a different pragmatic justification of induction, which amounts roughly to this: "Maybe induction does not work, but if anything does, induction will. Maybe there is no order in the universe, but if there is any (on any level), induction will eventually find it (on the next-highest level)." There is some merit to this approach, but there is also a problem with the word "eventually." Finally, there has been an attempt to dissolve the problem by showing that following our commonsense inductive rules is what is meant by rationality, and therefore no further justification is called for.

I wrote in the introduction that philosophy is not a guide to life, a branch of theology or mathematics, or merely a matter of being stoical in the face of adversity. Whatever the resolution of Hume's traditional problem of induction, it beautifully exemplifies the nature of philosophical inquiry. Once Hume enunciated his insight into induction (and causality, which we will treat later), it became impossible for anyone to think about induction in the same way again. No new facts or theorems or prescriptions were offered, just a sometimes scary realization that induction is not what it appears to be in our uncritical daily life, where our focus is usually on the eggs we need.

A Humerous induction:

MARTHA: On all my birthdays up to now I've been less than twenty-five years old. So by induction, on all my birthdays I'll be less than twenty-five years old.

Hume's analysis of the notion of causality is similarly unsettling. According to Hume, when we say "A causes B" we mean nothing more than that A and B are constantly conjoined, that in every instance we've examined, the event A has been followed by the event B. Since it's quite easy to imagine A not being followed by B, the connection between A and B cannot be a necessary or logical one. Causes and effects are discoverable by experience and not by a priori reasoning. Many people—including, of course, Kant—believe this.

Still, there are problems with this view of cause and effect. Consider, for example, scientific laws. Are they merely concise summaries of past "constant conjunctions" of A's and B's, descriptive restatements of A's being followed by B's? What makes it hard to maintain this view is, as Nelson Goodman has noted, that scientific laws, unlike accidental generalizations, seem to support counterfactual conditionals. (A counterfactual conditional is a statement of the form "If A were the case, then B would be the case," when in fact A is *not* the case.)

Thus the scientific law "All objects with a specific density greater than that of water sink when placed in water" supports the counterfactual conditional "If this nail had been placed in the water, it would have sunk." The accidental generalization "All the students in George's Math 5 class are functionally illiterate" does not, however, support the counterfactual conditional "If Martha were placed in George's Math 5 class, she would be functionally illiterate." Similarly, the accidental generalization "All bodies of pure arsenic have a mass of less than one ton" does not support counterfactual statements like "Two bodies of pure arsenic whose combined masses are more than one ton cannot be fused to form one body," or "If two such bodies were fused, the mass of the resulting body would still be less than one ton."

The ontological status of scientfic laws is thus not quite clear. They seem to be more than just summaries of constant conjunctions, since they support counterfactuals, yet they are certainly less than necessary or logical truths.

There is a story by Leo Rosten (1968) that is marginally relevant:

An insensitive oaf (a *bulvon*) was about to go out on a blind date and asked his Lothario of a friend for some advice. The friend responded, "I'll tell you a secret. Jewish girls love three topics of conversation: food, family, and philosophy. That's all you need to remember. To ask about a girl's tastes in food is to make her feel important. To ask about her family shows that your intentions are honorable. And to discuss philosophy with her shows you respect her intelligence.''

The *bulvon* was pleased. "Food, family, philosophy!''

He met the girl and blurted, "Hello. Do you like noodles?''

"Why, no'' said the startled girl.

"Do you have a brother?''

"No.''

The *bulvon* hesitated for just a moment: "Well, if you had a brother, would he like noodles?''

Medical people and biologists sometimes use "cause'' in a bizarre way. They reason that if x cures y, then lack of x must cause y. If dopamine, for example, lessens the tremors of Parkinson's disease, then lack of dopamine must cause it. If an antagonist of dopamine reduces the symptoms of schizophrenia, then an excess of it must cause schizophrenia. One is less likely to make this mistake when the situation is more mundane. Few people believe that since aspirin cures headaches, it must be the case that lack of aspirin in the bloodstream causes them.

Similar things can be said about some uses of "cause'' in the social sciences.

Two Australian aborigines were brought to this country and saw for the first time a waterskier winding and cavorting his way around a lake. "Why is the boat going so fast?" asked one of the aborigines. The second answered, "Because it is being chased by a madman on a string."

The Tortoise Came First?

In clarifying the structure of the first-cause argument for the existence of (a) God, Bertrand Russell cites the Hindu myth that the world rests on an elephant and the elephant rests on a tortoise. When asked about the tortoise, the Hindu replies, "Let's change the subject."

But let's *not* change the subject. Assuming *some* reasonable understanding of the word "cause," either everything has a cause or something does not. If everything has a cause, God does too. If there is something that does not have a cause, it may as well be the physical world as God or a tortoise.

The cogency of this reply to the first-cause argument is indicated by Saint Augustine's reaction to a version of it. When he was asked what God was doing before He made the world, he answered, "He was creating a hell for people who ask questions like that."

The natural-law argument for the existence of God has a similar structure and is thus open to a similar reply. The argument posits God as the lawgiver, the author of order and law in the natural world. Whatever power the argument has is greatly diminished by asking why God created the particular natural laws that He did. If He did it whimsically, for no reason at all, there is then something that is not subject to natural law; the chain of natural law is broken. On the other hand, if He had reasons for issuing the particular laws that He did, then God himself is subject to law and there is not much point in introducing Him as an intermediary in the first place.

There is a statistical "law of nature" that says that if you throw a pair of dice, you will get a two (one on each die) only about once in thirty-six throws. Many laws of nature are, of course, of this sort. Though they indicate an order or lawfulness on one level, this order or lawfulness exists only because of disorder or randomness on a lower level. Compare the second law of thermodynamics, which states that in any *closed* system, entropy (disorder, roughly), being more probable, is continually increasing. (Living things— little islands of order that replicate themselves, and from which more complex configurations can evolve—are not closed systems, and thus do not constitute a counterexample to the second law of thermodynamics. They eat, are warmed by the sun, etc.)

It is in fact hard, if not impossible, to imagine a *completely* random universe. It seems that in any universe there would necessarily be, on some level, some kind of order or lawfulness, even if only of a very Pickwickian sort. Even in a very messy universe one could describe the mess (assuming one were around, which is not likely) or enunciate some higher-order prediction to the effect that no lower-order predictions seem to work.

Why is it not termed a miracle when a freak gust of wind topples a single flowerpot from a tenth-story window and the flowerpot falls onto the head of a person walking on the sidewalk below, or when a faith healer ministers to a blind man who then becomes lame?

Constants of different sorts: Planck's constant, 55 mph speed limit, 3 ft. in a yard, π.

Laws of different sorts: Conservation of mass-energy, parking ordinance, Thou shalt not kill, Boyle's laws of gases.

One reasonable reaction to the refutation of the first-cause and natural-law arguments is to try to make sense of the first cause not only causing the second cause(s) but also causing itself—or, analogously, the most general law not only explaining the next most general law(s) but also explaining itself. Robert Nozick, in *Philosophical Explanations*, considers one such self-subsumptive principle, *P*, of the following type : Any lawlike statement having characteristic *C* is true. Principle *P* is used to explain why other, less general laws hold true: they hold true because they have characteristic *C*. What, however, explains why *P* holds true? The answer is that *P*, since it also has characteristic *C*, explains why it itself holds true. In short, *P*, if true, explains itself.

Even Nozick acknowledges that this "appears quite weird—a feat of legerdemain" (1981). Still, there are not, as he notes, many alternatives. The chain of causes (laws) is either finite or infinite. If it is finite, the most basic cause (most general law) either is a brute, arbitrary fact or is self-subsuming.

Self-subsuming principles need not be any deeper or of any higher order than what they explain. They could perhaps be handled by a variant of Kripke's theory of truth, in which statements attain their level naturally rather than being preassigned a fixed level, and in which self-referential statements sometimes receive truth values. (Perhaps even the oscillation associated with certain paradoxical statements—if they're true, they're false, which makes them true, which makes them false, etc.—could be given a physical meaning consistent with the notion of self-subsumption.)

Nozick writes also of certain yogic mystical exercises that help to bring about the experiential analogue of self-subsumption. He theorizes that "one of the acts the (male) yogis perform, during their experiences of being identical with infinitude, is auto-fellatio, wherein they have an intense and ecstatic experience of self-generation, of the universe and themselves turned back upon itself in a self-creation" (1981).

All this, of course, is contrary to Marxist theory. As Marx (Groucho) himself might have observed, "First Russell defines mathematics as the subject where we never know what we're talking about nor whether what we're saying is true, and now this Nozick joker says that the most basic laws of the universe have something to do with yogis playing with themselves; and yet they call *me* a comedian.''

Pascal once said, "To poke fun at philosophy is to be a philosopher'' (1966). Although this is not quite true—poking fun being a necessary but not a sufficient condition for being a philosopher—it and Groucho's imagined reaction to Russell and Nozick do suggest a deep resonance between humor and philosophy. Ideally, both activities require—in fact, presuppose—a free intelligence stepping back from roles, rules, and rote, in order to respond to the world with honesty and courage. Ideally.

Hume's traditional problem of induction aside (consider it solved, resolved, dissolved, or just ignored), there remains the problem of exactly which regularities in nature are projectable into the future. All samples of water so far examined (under normal atmospheric pressure) have been found to have a freezing point of 32°F; it thus seems reasonable to project this regular connection between being a water sample and having a freezing point of 32°F into the future. It is also true that all major economic depressions have occurred at the same time as large sunspots; yet in this case, it does not seem reasonable to project this regular connection between economic depressions and sunspots into the future.

Nelson Goodman has shown (1965) that the question of which regularities are projectable into the future is more problematical than these two examples indicate. Goodman's projectability paradox can be explained by considering the strange electrical terms "condulator" and "insuductor." A date in the future is selected, say January 1, 2010. Something is termed a condulator if it is a conductor and the time is before 2010, or if it is an insulator and the time is after January 1, 2010. Something is an insuductor, on the other hand, if it's an insulator and the time is before 2010, or if it's a conductor and the time is after January 1, 2010. Now let's consider the properties of copper wire. All samples of copper wire tested up to now (1984) have been conductors; we therefore feel we have good evidence that all copper wires are conductors of electricity. But, Goodman points out, all copper wires so far tested are also condulators: it seems as though we have just as good a body of evidence for the proposition that all copper wires are condulators (and hence insulators beginning in 2010).

Of course, a natural objection to these electrical terms "condulator" and "insuductor" is that they are defined in terms of the year 2010. But what if there really were a people who developed a language or scientific theory of which condulator/insuductor was a part? They could make the same charge against us. "Conductor," they could maintain, is an odd term, being defined as condulator before 2010 and insuductor afterward. "Insulator" is just as strange, being insuductor before 2010 and condulator from then on.

More generally, it is not just these isolated terms but the languages, theories, and worldviews of which they're a part that structure the world and its observers in incommensurable ways, and thus lead to very different expectations about the future. One could, for example, rig up two electric chairs, one with copper wiring and the other with asbestos wiring, and have the leading scientists from each side sit in the chair of their choice on January 1, 2010.

Goodman's original example concerned the odd color terms "grue" and "bleen" and is usually referred to as the grue-bleen paradox. An object is grue if green before 2010, say, or blue afterward. Bleen is defined similarly, and it's stressed that whatever evidence we have for all emeralds being green is also evidence for all emeralds being grue. Grue-bleeners, however, can point out that it is really "blue" and "green" that are the strange color terms, the latter being grue before 2010 or bleen afterward, and the former being bleen before 2010 or grue afterward. Of course, an indefinite number of such puzzles can be generated—republicrats and democans (2010 could be a cataclysmic year)—but how to get around them is not completely clear.

Another intriguing paradox is due to Carl Hempel (1965). His "raven" paradox, so called because it is usually illustrated with ravens, can be easily stated. Suppose we want to confirm the statement "All ravens are black." We go out, look for ravens, and check to see if they are black. We believe that if we observe enough instances of black ravens, we will have confirmed (not necessarily conclusively verified) the statement "All ravens are black." But by elementary logic, "All ravens are black" is logically equivalent to "All non-black objects are nonravens." Since the statements are equivalent, any observation that confirms one confirms the other. But pink flamingos, orange shirts, and chartreuse lampshades are all instances of nonblack objects, and thus tend to confirm the statement "All nonblack objects are nonravens"; therefore they must also confirm "All ravens are black." Hence we arrive at the curious position of having pink flamingos, orange shirts, and chartreuse lampshades confirming the statement that all ravens are black!

What is the problem? Well, it still is not clear to people. Two quick points should be made, however. One is that merely amassing instances of a statement is not enough to confirm it. The second is that nonravens and nonblack objects are much more numerous than ravens and black objects. Perhaps we could understand pink flamingos, orange shirts, and chartreuse lampshades as confirming, but only very slightly, the two equivalent statements above— not as much, in fact as a black raven would.

Similarly, to confirm "All congressmen have problems with grammar" one could go out, look for people who speak grammatically, check to see that they're not congressmen, and obtain some minuscule confirmation for the statement. More conclusive confirmation for it, though, would come from attending congressional hearings.

It is hard to say in general when an observation confirms (again, not necessarily conclusively verifies) a statement. Hempel considered some conditions that the notion of confirmation might be expected to satisfy. Two obvious ones, it seemed, were (1) If an observation o confirms a statement h and h implies another statement k, then o confirms k; and (2) If an observation o confirms a statement k and another statement h implies k, then o confirms h.

But from (1) and (2) we can derive the following: Let h = the theory of relativity, and k = the thermostat is above 80°. Then its being hot in the room tends to confirm k (on any intuitive understanding of confirmation), and thus tends by (2) to confirm the compound statement (h and k)

(symbolically, $h \wedge k$), since $h \wedge k$ implies k. Hence, by (1) h is confirmed, since $h \wedge k$ implies h. Thus we conclude that its being hot in the room confirms the theory of relativity! Something is obviously wrong with (1) and (2) together. (2) seems especially suspect, but some (weakened) version of (2) is certainly often used, and is necessary in the everyday practice of science. Even (1) is not always the case.

Let us consider one final oddity. Ever since Plato, knowledge has been taken by many philosophers to be justified true belief. A subject S is said to know a proposition P if (a) P is true; (b) S believes that P is true; and (c) S is justified in believing that P is true. Edmund L. Gettier has shown (1963) that these three ancient conditions are not sufficient to ensure knowledge.

To show this, suppose that George and Martha are the only applicants for a certain job at Lower Slobovia State University. Suppose further that George has strong evidence for the following compound proposition:

(1) Martha is the person who will be hired, and Martha has unruly hair this morning. George's evidence for (1) might be that the chairman of the department informed him that Martha's specialty, unlike George's, was the one the department had been looking for. Further, he could see that the department chairman and Martha had established an early rapport despite her unruly hair—while the chairman barely spoke to him, hurried him out of his office, and

muttered something nasty-sounding to his secretary that made her laugh derisively.

Proposition (1) implies:

(2) The person who gets this job has unruly hair. George sees that (1) implies (2) and thus accepts (2) on the basis of (1), for which, as we've seen, he has strong evidence. Clearly George is justified in believing that (2) is true.

So far, so good. But suppose that, unknown to George, he, not Martha, will get the job. (The chairman, imagine, has a strange psychology.) Also unknown to George, his hair was ruffled by the fan in the elevator, causing his cowlick to stand up. Proposition (2) is thus true even though (1) from which it was inferred is false. Now all the following are true: (a) (2) is true; (b) George believes that (2) is true; and (c) George is justified in believing that (2) is true. But, of course, it is quite clear that George does not *know* (2), since (2) is true in virtue of George's own unruly hair, of which he is unaware. Thus justified, true belief does not constitute knowledge.

If justified true belief does not constitute knowledge, the question remains: What does? One answer, due to the philosophers Fred Dretske and Robert Nozick, involves the notion of subjunctive or counterfactual conditionals. They state that S knows P if (a) P is true; (b) S believes P; (c) If P weren't true, S would not believe P; and (d) If P were true (but other minor things were different), S would still believe P. For example, by these criteria George does not know "The person who gets the job has unruly hair." If the proposition in question weren't true—say, George's hair was not accidently ruffled by the fan in the elevator but he still got the job—George would still believe the proposition. Thus condition (c) is not met, and George cannot be said to know the proposition. (Condition [d] handles other related difficulties.)

Since these four conditions, it can be argued, are sufficient for knowledge, and since such counterfactual and subjunctive conditionals are also helpful in the analysis of scientific law (and notions like "possible worlds"), why not declare the war over and decree that these problems are resolved? The reason, for many philosophers, is that the analysis of these conditionals is at least as problematic as the notions they are meant to clarify.

Truths, Half-Truths, and Statistics

Benjamin Disraeli coined the phrase "Lies, damn lies, and statistics," and the phrase (as well as the sentiment) has lasted—though I like "Truths, half-truths, and statistics" better. In any case, even relatively simple applications of statistics can cause problems, not to mention the horrors associated with things like the often misinterpreted SPSS computer software (Statistical Programs for the Social Sciences).

Probability and statistics, like geometry and mathematics in general, come in two flavors: pure and applied. Pure probability theory is a formal calculus whose primitive terms are uninterpreted and whose axioms are neither true nor false. These axioms originally arise from and are made meaningful by real-life interpretations of terms like "probability," "event," and "random sample." The problem with applying probability and statistics is often not in the formal mathematical manipulations themselves, but in the appropriateness of the application, the validity of the interpretation, and indeed the "reasonableness" of the whole enterprise. This latter activity goes beyond mathematics into the sometimes murky realm of common sense and the philosophy of science (grue-bleen, ravens, etc.). Even though 1 plus 1 equals 2, one glass of water plus one glass of popcorn does not equal two glasses of mixture. The mathematics is fine, the application is not.

MARTHA: What did you get for the density of the block, George?

GEORGE: Well, it weighed about 17 pounds and had a volume of about 29 cubic feet, so I guess the density is .58620689551 pounds per cubic foot. This calculator's really swell.

Babe Ruth and Lou Gehrig played baseball for the New York Yankees. Suppose Ruth had a higher batting average than Gehrig for the first half of the season. Suppose further that during the second half of the season Ruth continued to hit for a higher batting average than Gehrig. Is it nevertheless possible for Gehrig's batting average for the entire season to be higher than Ruth's batting average for the entire season? The fact that I've used up a paragraph asking the question indicates that the answer is yes, but how can it be?

One way it can be is for Ruth during the first half of the season to hit for an average of .344, getting 55 hits in 160 times at bat; while Gehrig during this same time hits for an average of .342, getting 82 hits for 240 times at bat. During the second half of the season Ruth's average is .250, since he gets 60 hits in 240 times at bat; whereas Gehrig's is

.238, as he gets 38 hits in 160 times at bat. Nevertheless for the season as a whole, Gehrig's average of .300 is higher than Ruth's average of .287.

Thus even the third-grade notion of an average can be misused, not to mention (as I already have) things like complicated multidimensional analyses of variance.

If Waldo comes from country x, 30 percent of whose citizens have a certain characteristic, then if we know nothing else about Waldo, it seems reasonable to assume that there is a 30 percent probability that Waldo shares this characteristic. If we later discover that Waldo belongs to a certain ethnic group 80 percent of whose members in the region comprising countries x, y, and z have the characteristic in question, what now are Waldo's chances of sharing this characteristic? What if we subsequently determine that Waldo belongs to a nation-x-wide organization only 15 percent of whose members have this characteristic? What now can we conclude, with all this information, about Waldo's chances of having the characteristic in question?

Wittgenstein writes about a man who, not being certain of an item he reads in the newspaper, buys a hundred copies of the paper to reassure himself of its truth. Given the extent to which news-people and the media report each other's reports, checking in several different papers or periodicals is not much more intelligent.

News release: Abortions are becoming so popular in some countries that the waiting time to get one is lengthening rapidly. Experts predict that at this rate there will soon be a one-year wait to get an abortion.

The projection of "trends" linearly into the future is often about as reliable as this "news release."

Most automobile accidents occur close to home, so we can see that near one's home is the most dangerous place to drive.

Very few accidents occur when one is driving over 95 mph, so it's clear that driving this fast is actually quite safe.

It is a surprising, almost counterintuitive, fact that if just 23 people are chosen at random from a telephone directory, the probability is .5 (chances are about 50-50) that at least two of them will have the same birthday. Recently someone was trying to explain this oddity on a television talk show. The incredulous host thought the man must be wrong, and so asked the studio audience how many people had the same birthday as he did, say March 19. When nobody in the audience of about 150 people responded, the host felt vindicated and the guest felt embarrassed. Actually, the question the host had raised was very different fromn the one the guest had been discussing. It turns out that a randomly selected group of 253 people is required in order for the probability to be .5 that at least one member of the group has any *specific* birthdate (such as March 19); a group of only 23 people is required for the probability to be .5 that there is *some* birthdate in common.

This is a specific instance of a very general phenomenon. Even though any particular event of a certain sort may be quite rare, that *some* event of that sort will occur is not rare at all. The science writer Martin Gardner illustrates this point with the story of a spinner that is equally likely to stop at any of the twenty-six letters of the alphabet. If the spinner is twirled 100 times and the results recorded, the probability of any *particular* three-letter word, say "cat," appearing is quite small, whereas the probability of *some* three-letter word appearing is very high.

Columbus discovered the New World in 1492, while his fellow Italian Enrico Fermi discovered the atomic world in 1942. John Kennedy, elected president in 1960 and assassinated in office, had a Lincoln for a secretary, while Abraham Lincoln, elected president in 1860 and assassinated in office, had a Kennedy for a secretary. As Gardner has noted, the acronym formed by the planets listed in order—Mercury, Venus, Earth, Mars, Jupiter, Saturn, Uranus, Neptune, Pluto—is M V E M J <u>S U N</u> P, while that for the months is J F M A M J J A S O N D. In each case we have an unlikely happening whose type, while almost impossible to specify precisely, is quite likely to have some instances. This has some relevance to evolution. That a particular branch should have evolved in a particular way is quite improbable. That some branch should have evolved in something like the way in question is much less so.

The probability of getting at least one head on two flips of a coin is .75. The chances of rain tomorrow are 75 percent. I think the odds of George's marrying Martha are 3 to 1. Does "probability = .75" mean the same thing in each of the above cases? The preceding discussion concerning unlikely coincidences might be summarized aphoristically as, "It's very improbable that no improbable event will occur." Are both uses of "improbable" in this statement the same?

Duhem, Poincaré, and the Poconos-Catskill Diet

Even in the best of circumstances, applying the classical canons of scientific inference is not always straightforward. If a certain hypothesis H implies or makes more likely some event I, then if that event I occurs, H is strengthened; whereas if the event I does not occur, H is weakened or refuted. The raven and confirmation paradoxes demonstrated that I's occurrence (the sighting of pink flamingoes, say) does not necessarily strengthen H (the statement that all ravens are black). The French philosopher Pierre Duhem, on the other hand, showed that I's *non*occurrence does not necessarily refute or weaken H either.

To see this, consider the Poconos-Catskill diet. Dr. Poconos, a Greek doctor from Pennsylvania, and Dr. Catskill, an Irish doctor from New York, prescribe two large servings of pastitsio (a meat, cheese, and noodle dish), three pieces of baklava, and four beers for every meal. They guarantee that after one week on this diet, a person will lose at least six pounds. George and Martha go on this diet and gain nine pounds in one week. Must Drs. Poconos and Catskill retract their hypothesis H, that the diet is effective, given that I, the loss of at least six pounds, did not occur? Of course not. They could maintain that a host of other auxiliary, but tacit, hypotheses failed, and not their pet hypothesis H, the Poconos-Catskill diet. Maybe the pastitsio was too heavily salted or not salted enough, maybe George and Martha slept fourteen hours a day during the week, or maybe the meals were not spaced correctly.

Thus the nonoccurrence of I can never by itself refute H, since there will always be scapegoats—auxiliary hypotheses to blame. What is being tested is never just "H implies I," but rather "H and H_I and H_2 and H_3 and . . . implies I," where the ellipsis indicates indefinitely many auxiliary hypotheses. I's nonoccurrence thus indicates only that either H or (at least) one of the auxiliary hypotheses must be false, not necessarily that H is false.

Willard Van Orman Quine has gone even further than Duhem in maintaining that experience never forces the rejection of individual statements. He conceives of science as an integrated web of statements, procedures, and formalisms in contact with reality only at its edges. Any impact of the world on the web is distributed throughout the web, with no part (even logic) being absolutely immune and no part having to bear the brunt of that impact alone. Adjustments can always be made in the whole web to accommodate the experience, but there is no unique way to make these adjustments—simplicity, efficiency, and tradition being some of the criteria for a good web (science). We could thus accept that the Poconos-Catskill diet is an effective weight-loss program (as commercials often phrase it), but we would have to make fairly drastic changes in the rest of our web.

Similarly, in physics, if one wanted, for whatever reason, to accept some bizarre statement as true, one could do so by suitably and radically altering other statements, the interpretation of certain physical terms, and so on. This is related to the traditional problem in the philosophy of science of where to draw the line between empirical physics and a priori geometry. If one insists that geometry must be Euclidean, one's physics (in certain astronomical contexts, say) becomes quite strange, with accelerations and forces that don't make sense by traditional theoretical standards. An alternative is to switch to an appropriate non-Euclidean geometry that makes the physics simpler, but which itself seems quite counterintuitive at first. Which geometry-physics combination to use depends on one's purposes and is to some extent a matter of convention, as Henri Poincaré first noted (1913).

Of course, not just physics but any complicated phenomenon, especially one that involves human interaction, admits of many different and incompatible interpretations, each consistent with reality. The differing "theories" of their particular marriage entertained by a husband and wife, for example, often manifest this incomparability, as does the following Sufi story adapted from Masud Farzan's *Another Way of Laughter*:

Since a Roman scholar was visiting Timur's court, the emperor asked the Mulla to ready himself for a battle of wits with the scholar.

The Mulla piled books with fictitious but impressive-sounding titles on his donkey, books such as *The Theory of Universal Bifurcants*, *Erosion and Civilization*, *A Critique of Tolerant Purity*, and *Social Origins of Mental De-activation*.

On the day of the contest, the Mulla appeared in court with his donkey and books. His native wit and intelligence overwhelmed the Roman scholar, who finally decided to test the Mulla's knowledge of theoretical matters. The Roman scholar held up one finger.

The Mulla answered with two fingers.

The Roman held up three fingers.

The Mulla responded with four.

The scholar showed his whole palm, to which Mulla responded with a closed fist.

The scholar then opened his briefcase and took out an egg. The Mulla responded by digging an onion out of his pocket.

The Roman said, "What's your evidence?

The Mulla answered, "*The Theory of Universal Bifurcants*, *A Critique of Tolerant Purity*," etc.

When the Roman sputtered that he'd never even heard of those titles, the Mulla responded: "Of course you haven't. Look and you will see hundreds of books you've never read."

The Roman looked and was so impressed that he conceded defeat. Since no one had understood any of this, later, after refreshments had been served, the emperor leaned over and asked the Roman scholar the meaning of it all.

"He is a brilliant man, this Mulla," the Roman explained. "When I held up one finger, meaning that there was only one God, he held up two to say that He created heaven and earth. I held up three fingers, meaning the conception-life-death cycle of man, to which the Mulla responded by showing four fingers, indicating that the body is composed of four elements—earth, air, water, and fire."

"Well then, what about the egg and the onion?" the emperor pressed.

"The egg was the symbol of the earth (the yolk) surrounded by the heavens. The Mulla produced an onion, indicating the layers of heavens about the earth. I asked him to support this claim to assign the same number of layers of heavens as there are layers of onion skin, and he supported his claim by all those learned books of which I alas am ignorant. Your Mulla is a very learned man indeed." The dejected Roman then departed.

The emperor next asked the Mulla about the debate. He replied, "It was easy, Your Majesty. When he lifted a finger of defiance to me, I held up two, meaning I'd poke both his eyes out. When he held up three fingers indicating, I'm sure, that he'd deliver three kicks, I returned his threat by threatening four kicks. His whole palm, of course, meant a slap in my face, to which I responded with my clenched fist. Seeing I was serious, he began to be friendly and offered me an egg, so I offered him my onion."

Whether Mulla or Roman scholar was "right" is a matter of convention or tradition. As noted, conventionalism is the view that scientific laws are to a significant extent disguised conventions that reflect a decision, for one reason or other, to adopt one of various possible descriptions of a phenomenon. To return to physics, in some cases to ask if one event precedes another makes as much sense as asking if New York is really to the right of Chicago.

George Carlin once listed six reasons for doing something or other: I, b, III, four, E, vi. Notation, though clearly a matter of convention, is crucial. Imagine trying to explain even some elementary mathematics, such as the quadratic formula, without good notation.

If the story of the Mulla and the Roman seems too far-fetched, imagine a modern physicist trying to explain to an Australian aborigine that neutrinos have no mass, or something about the properties of quarks and black holes.

Reductionism, Fallibilism, and Opportunism

There are, of course, in addition to conventionalism many other "isms" in the philosophy of science, some of which should at least be mentioned. The most common of these is opportunism, as illustrated by the following well-known story:

MARTHA: What are you doing out by the streetlight, George?

GEORGE: I'm looking for my car keys.

MARTHA: But you dropped them on the grass near the bushes.

GEORGE: I know, but the light is better out here.

The following story due to Leo Rosten (1968) makes the same point, and also says something about the organization and contents of this book:

A famous rabbi was asked by an admiring student "How is it you always have a perfect parable for any topic?"

The rabbi smiled and said "I'll answer with a parable," and told this story:

Once there was a lieutenant in the tsar's army who, riding through a small shtetl, noticed a hundred chalked circles on the side of a barn, each one with a bullet hole in the center. The astonished lieutenant stopped the first passerby and inquired about all the bullseyes.

The passerby sighed. "Oh that's Shepsel, the shoemaker's son. He's a little peculiar."

"I don't care. Anyone who's that good a shot . . ."

"You don't understand," interrupted the passerby. "You see, first Shepsel shoots and then he draws the chalk circle."

The rabbi smiled. "That's the way it is with me. I don't look for a parable to fit the subject. I introduce only subjects for which I have parables."

Behaviorism is the philosophy of social science doctrine to the effect that psychological functioning is definable in terms of overt behavioral manifestations. It, together with a mindless respect for statistical formalism, has led to the publishing of whole barrels full of trivial research of the following form: If property x (humor, say) is operationally defined in this way (number of chuckles elicited by a book of cartoons), and property y (self-sufficiency, say) is operationally defined in this way (number of yes answers on some "self-sufficiency questionnaire"), then the correlation coefficient between x and y is .621 (at least for students in Prof. George's 8:30 psychology class).

The existence of boredom implies the falsity of behaviorism, but the details of the derivation bore me.

Behaviorism is a type of reductionism, the latter being any doctrine that claims to reduce what is apparently more sophisticated and complex to what is less so. Sometimes, of course, this is possible; large parts of genetics can be reduced to molecular biology, and some parts of thermodynamics to statistical mechanics, for example. Sometimes this reduction is not possible, at least not in any natural manner.

Consider, for example, clocks or can openers. (I wonder if the preceding seven-word sentence has ever appeared in print before?) A clock is any device for keeping time, a can opener any device for opening cans. To characterize these objects in purely physical terms, to reduce all talk of clocks and can openers to the language of physics, would be a pointless (though theoretically possible) endeavor. Imagine what sort of physical description could encompass all and only sundials, grandfather clocks, wristwatches, digital clocks, etc. Any such purely physical description would be a messy, unsystematic hodgepodge of ad hoc physical statements, and thus would offer no illumination on the purposes or identification of clocks or can openers.

Conversely, just as it is pointless though theoretically possible to describe clocks and can openers in purely physical terms, it is pointless though theoretically possible to eliminate theoretical physical terms like "neutrino," "guard," and "covalent bond" and replace them with an unsystematic hodgepodge of ordinary, everyday observational statements containing terms like "red," "cold," and "hard." The predictive and organizational strength of scientific theories would, of course, be lost if this were done. Carl Hempel (1963) has shown explicitly how to rid science of theoretical terms (and thus cripple it) using Craig's theorem, a well-known result from mathematical logic. For some reason, though, one never hears this referred to as reducing physics to the "theory of common sense."

Richard Dawkins in his book *The Selfish Gene* seems to argue that our genes try to perpetuate themselves by fashioning our actions in such a way as to assure their own survival. Human behavior and culture is, on this sociobiological view, largely determined by our genes' desire for self-preservation. This reductionist account certainly needs supplementation. Note, for example, that different cultures with essentially the same genetic pool engender quite different behaviors. Note, too, that we can carry the reduction even further. One might argue that it is not our genes that are selfish, but a particular chemical bond in the genes. Our actions are not determined by our genes after all, but by a chemical bond in them that is trying to perpetuate itself. I am being simplistic, but so is the thesis as it is usually presented.

x can be explained in terms of *y*. *y* does not have property *P*. So *x* does not have *P*.

The greenness of grass, the blueness of the sky, the flesh tones of a human face can all be explained in terms of (the properties of) atoms—frequencies and so on. But atoms themselves are not colored. So grass is not green, the sky is not blue, and faces are not flesh-colored.

Similar arguments have been used to show that values, ethics, ideals, even intentions and beliefs, are illusions.

There is a story about a London man who spent his life looking around and recording everything he noticed in a series of notebooks. He directed that after his death these observation notebooks be forwarded to the Royal Society, so that scientists there could use them to fashion a new scientific theory.

Though some people still think that science advances in this way (consider some behaviorist research, e.g.), most realize that scientific research needs first a focus or problem; next, assumptions and hypotheses; and only then, new observations. Scientific pronouncements should be supported (or at least supportable), and, as the English philosopher Sir Karl Popper has stressed, they must be capable of being shown false. They must be falsifiable or fallible, at least in principle.

When a plane crashes, many people remark that these sorts of things always happen in threes. This belief is, as stated, completely unfalsifiable. Even if the next crash, two months later, occurs in Peru, and the third involves a small private plane in an Arkansas cornfield, these people can still maintain that they have some special insight into aeronautical malfunctioning, or, more commonly, that "everyone" has this knowledge. Similar things can be said about remarks like "Whatever God wills, happens."

Popper has criticized Marxism and Freudianism for being too much like the above theory of plane crashes—that is, for not being falsifiable and thus not being real sciences. He has in mind moves of the following sort: A Marxist predicts that the "ruling class" will respond in such and such an exploitive way to some crisis; when it doesn't, this is attributed to some sneaky, co-opting policy of the ruling class. Similarly, an orthodox psychoanalyst might predict a certain kind of neurotic behavior; when his patient doesn't behave in this way, but in a quite contrary way, this is attributed to a "reaction-formation." Popper does not quite say so, but he hints that Freud is a fraud and that Karl Marx makes less sense than Groucho.

More generally, Popper is opposed to historicism, the doctrine that there are immutable "laws of development" that govern the historical process and allow long-term social forecasts. One argument for Popper's position is that scientific advances that obviously greatly affect social development are not predictable. How could someone predict Descartes's discovery (or invention, if you like) of analytic geometry, or Einstein's discovery-invention of relativity theory? Imagine a "futurologist" of the sixteenth (or nineteenth) century predicting the development of analytic geometry (or relativity theory): if such a prediction had any detailed content, it would in a sense already be fulfilled and thus not be a prediction at all.

Less well known than Popper's ideas on falsifiability is his concern with the notion of randomness, the topic of the next section.

Randomness and the Berry Task

GEORGE: What's Waldo's phone number? I always forget.

MARTHA: Let me see. The Goodmans have 2 children, the Frankels have 3, the Passows have 7 dogs (though Myrtle may be pregnant), the Youngs have 2 kids from his first marriage, 1 from hers, and 3 of their own, and the Sturms have 9 pets in all. Waldo's number is 237-2139.

GEORGE: Thanks. It's a good thing I know the area code.

(1) 00100100100100100100100100100100100100100 . . .

(2) 10110101011011011010101101010101011010110101010 . . .

(3) 10001011011011000101011001011110100101101010 . . .

Why is it that the first sequence of 0s and 1s is likely to be termed orderly or patterned, the last sequence random or patternless, and the second somewhere in between? Trying to answer this simple question will lead to a definition of randomness, an important insight in the philosophy of science, and an alternative proof of Godel's incompleteness theorem.

Returning to the question, note that the first sequence has an easily expressed pattern: two 0s, then a 1, repeated indefinitely. The third sequence has no such pattern; while in the second sequence, 0s always alternate with either one or two 1s, but the occurrence of one or two seems patternless.

With examples like this in mind, the American computer scientist Gregory Chaitin and the Russian mathematician A. N. Kolmogorov defined the *complexity* of a sequence of 0s and 1s to be the length of the *shortest* computer program that will generate the sequence in question. For the sake of uniformity, assume that the language of the program is coded into a sequence of 0s and 1s so that the program itself can be considered a sequence of 0s and 1s. Thus we can take the length of a program to be simply the number of 0s and 1s in it. If the program is the shortest one to generate a given sequence, the program's length in bits (0s or 1s) is the complexity of that given sequence.

A program that generates the first sequence above will just be a translation into machine language of the following recipe: two 0s, then a 1, repeated x times. This program should be quite short compared to the length of the sequence, which, let us assume, is 10 trillion bits; and thus the sequence has, despite its length, a complexity of only 1 million bits, say.

A program that generates the second sequence would be a translation of the following: one 0 alternating with either one or two 1s, the pattern of 1s being one-two-one-one-two-two-two-one-one-two-one-one-one-two-one-two-one-one . . . If the second sequence were very long, say 10 trillion bits again, and this pattern continued, any program that generated it would have to be quite long to give the pattern of the intervening 1s. Still, the shortest such program, considered as a sequence of 0s and 1s itself, would be considerably shorter than the 10-trillion-bit sequence it was generating. The complexity of this sequence thus might be only 5 trillion, for example.

With the third sequence the situation is different. The sequence, let us assume, is so disorderly throughout its 10-trillion-bit length that no program we might use to generate it would be any shorter than the sequence itself. Since all the program can do in this case is just list the bits in the sequence, there is no way it can be shortened. Such a program, itself expressed in bits, is at least as long as the sequence it is supposed to generate, whose complexity thus is at least 10 trillion. The sequence is random.

More formally, we can define a sequence to be *random* if its complexity is (roughly) equal to its length; that is, if the shortest program capable of generating it has (roughly) the same length as the sequence itself. A sequence is then not random if its complexity is less than its length. Sequence (3) is random on this account, while sequences (1) and (2) are not. Two important consequences of these definitions are (a) If two sequences of different lengths are random, the longer one is more complex; and (b) For any given whole number x, the vast majority of sequences of bits of length x are random; there are only a relatively few low-complexity ones of any given length.

Intelligibility or precision: to combine the two is impossible.
                                                      Bertrand Russell

Attempts have been made to apply these formal notions of complexity and randomness more generally. A. Solomonoff theorized, for example, that a scientist's observations could be coded up into a sequence of 0s and 1s. The goal of science then would be to find short programs (algorithms, recipes) capable of generating (deriving, predicting) these observations. Such a program, so the story goes, would be a scientific theory, and the shorter it was, relative to the phenomena it predicted, the more powerful it would be. Random events would not be predictable, except in a very fractured sense by a program that simply listed them.

There are, of course, serious problems in trying to extend the use of these technical notions to more general contexts. Where do these sequences of 0s and 1s come from in the first place? Exactly how are observations to be coded into a sequence of bits? Or prediction sequences decoded? What relation do they have to other significant categories? (Recall the sportscaster in a hurry: "And now for the baseball scores—6 to 2, 4 to 1, 8 to 5, 7 to 3, 5 to 0, and in a real slug-fest, 14 to 12.") It is impossible to divorce these sequences from the way they are obtained and employed, and from the human interests and values that led to their discovery and explanatory significance. Without this supporting scientific and cultural background, the sequences are meaningless.

Wittgenstein once remarked, "That Newtonian mechanics *can* be used to describe the world tells nothing about the world. But this does tell us something—that it can be used to describe the world *in the way in which we do in fact use it.*" The same thing can be said about scientific theories conceived of as programs that generate predictions: the way in which we do in fact use them *is* their scientific content. The reductionist tendency to be seduced by the simplicity and exactitude of this account of scientific theories as prediction-generating programs, and the consequent desire to declare that science is nothing but the study of such programs, should be resisted.

Ah but a man's reach should exceed his grasp,
Or what's a heaven for.   —*Robert Browning*

The formal notions of complexity and randomness, though they suffer from the limitations discussed above, are nevertheless often suggestive and useful. Chaitin has employed them and a detoxified version of the Berry paradox to give an alternative proof of Godel's first incompleteness theorem. Since the proof sheds a somewhat different light on this famous result, a sketch of it follows.

The Berry paradox, first published in 1908 by Bertrand Russell and attributed to a Mr. Berry, asks one to consider the following task: "Find the smallest whole number that requires in order to be specified more words than there are in this sentence." Examples such as the number of hairs on my head, the number of different states of a Rubik cube, and the speed of light in centimeters per decade, each specify, using fewer than the number of words in the given sentence, some particular whole number. The paradoxical nature of the task becomes clear when we realize that the Berry sentence specifies a particular whole number that, by definition, it contains too few words to specify.

What yields a paradox in English can be modified (detoxified) to yield a statement in a formal system that cannot be proved, and whose negation also cannot be proved. Consider a formal axiomatic system of arithmetic expressed in some formal language that contains symbols for addition, multiplication, and so on. This system—formulas, axioms of arithmetic, rules of inference—can be encoded into a sequence of 0s and 1s, a binary program P whose length in bits is $L(P)$. We can then conceive of a computer executing this program and over time generating from it the theorems of the system (encoded, of course, in bits). Stated a little differently, the program P generates sequences of bits that we interpret as the translations of statements in arithmetic, statements that the formal system has proven.

Now we ask whether the system is complete. For every arithmetic statement A, is it the case that either A or its negation, $\sim A$, will always be a theorem? (Is the sequence of bits associated with either A or $\sim A$ eventually generated by the computer?)

To see that the answer to this question is "No," we make a crucial alteration of the Berry sentence: we replace "that requires," a metalevel notion expressed in English, by "that can be proved to require," an object-level notion expressible in terms of 0s and 1s. (We assume that enough arithmetic is included in the original formal system to permit "talk," via some reasonable code involving 0s and 1s, of notions like provability, complexity, etc. within the system.)

Recalling that the complexity of a sequence of bits is the length of the shortest program needed to generate the sequence, we find that even the altered Berry task is impossible, though not paradox-inducing: "Find—that is, generate—a sequence of bits that can be proved to be of complexity greater than the number of bits in this program." (Again, enough arithmetic is assumed to be included in the original formal system to allow, via some sort of coding, for the self-reference of "in this program.") The program cannot generate such a sequence, since any sequence that the arithmetic program P generates must, by definition of complexity, be of complexity less than P itself is. Stated alternatively, there is a limit to the complexity of the sequences (translations of arithmetic statements) generated (proved) by P. That limit is, by the definition of complexity, the length, $L(P')$, of the shortest program encoding P.

Since a sequence is random if the length of any program generating it is at least as long as the sequence itself, we can further conclude that a formal system can generate a random sequence only if the sequence is less complex than the sequence encoding the system. That is, the only random sequences that the arithmetic system P can generate are necessarily less complex than P.

Hence we finally get to the undecidable statements that Godel promises us. Take g to be a random sequence of bits of complexity greater than that of P encoded into bits. This is always possible, since for any whole number x, most sequences of length x are random. Then the statement G: "g is random," properly encoded into bits, is unprovable by the system P. (Remember, "random" is defined in terms of "complexity," which is defined in terms of lengths of programs, all of which talk can be translated into arithmetic and then via code into a sequence of bits. Thus the statement "g is random" can be translated into a sequence of bits.) P cannot generate the sequence that is the translation of "g is random" for the reason discussed above; the sequence is too complex. Neither can P generate the sequence that represents the negation of "g is random," because g is random; since the axioms of P are true and the rules of inference preserve truth, only true statements can be proved. Therefore G can be neither proved nor disproved.

Godel's theorem can thus be interpreted as a consequence of the limited complexity of any formal arithmetic system, a limitation affecting human minds as well as machine programs. There is not the temptation, on this interpretation of the theorem, to dismiss many of the goals of artificial intelligence as impossible in principle, since machines cannot "step outside themselves" to the metalevel. This latter attempted refutation of mind-as-machine is rendered superficially plausible by more-standard proofs of Godel's theorem. Lastly, Chaitin's proof suggests that progress in mathematics is at times not so different from progress in other sciences. Instead of looking for new facts, one looks for new, true, independent axioms whose addition will make the relevant formal systems (or rather their translations into bits) more complex.

Determinism and Smart Computers

Although falsifiability and verifiability (testability for short) are important properties, it is unwise to be too rigid in interpreting these terms or too hasty in rejecting any pronouncements that are not testable (under any interpretation). Metaphysics is untestable and, as Friedrich Waissman responded in countering some zealous logical positivists, "To believe that metaphysics is nonsense is nonsense."

The metaphysical doctrines of determinism and indeterminism are certainly not testable in any strong sense. How is one to test that every event is determined, or that at least one event is not, *whatever* is meant by "determined"? Certain stronger, more precise theses *can* be formulated and refuted, though. Consider, for example, provable determinism, which maintains that every question in an appropriate language of science can be decided one way or the other on the basis of certain physical and mathematical laws. This is simply false by Godel's theorem, since incompleteness infects even formalized physical theories that include arithmetic in their formalization. A doctrinaire determinist can still maintain that the answer to every question is "determined" by "states of affairs," but not that every answer can be proved to follow from the given physical laws and mathematical theories.

Consider a computer, the "IBM-Cyber-007-know-it-all-smarty-pants," into which has been programmed (in some suitable language) the most complete scientific knowledge of the day, the initial conditions of all particles, and elaborate mathematical techniques and formulas. Imagine further that "know-it-all" answers only Yes or No questions, and that its output device is constructed in such a way that a Yes answer turns off an attached lightbulb and a No answer turns it on. If one asks this impressive machine something about the external world, the machine will respond, let us assume, flawlessly. However, if one asks it if its lightbulb will be on in one hour, "know-it-all" is stumped and cannot answer either way. This question, at least, is "undetermined" by the laws and axioms of its program (although an onlooking computer might be able to answer it).

Related to the "know-it-all" computer is the following phenomenon: In predicting what a person will decide, it is often very important to keep this predictive "information" secret from the person deciding. The scare quotes around "information" are meant to indicate that this peculiar type of information loses its value, becomes obsolete, if given to the person involved; it changes the person. The information, while it may be correct and true, is not universal. The onlooker and the deciding agent (compare "know-it-all") have complementary viewpoints. As D. M. MacKay has written, "To us, our choice is logically indeterminate until we make it. For us, choosing is not something to be observed or predicted, but to be done."

It is suggestive that in quantum mechanics, where indeterminism and subject-object interaction also play a crucial role, we also have the phenomenon of complementary viewpoints. A scientist might know the position of a particle, but that knowledge is incompatible with knowledge of the particle's momentum since, as the Heisenberg uncertainty principle states, the process of determining one necessarily affects the other.

Statistical laws have been around for a long time and may reflect either our ignorance of things or the nature of things. In philosophical parlance, they may reflect either an epistemic or a metaphysical condition. As far as microphysical phenomena go, quantum mechanics points to the latter conclusion. There is a fundamentally and irreducibly probabilistic aspect to atomic and subatomic happenings; some phenomena simply are random. Whether this microphysical indeterminism somehow percolates "up" through the structured complexity of the human (or inhuman) brain, resulting in free will, is an open question.

In any case, just as the mathematical existence of long random sequences of bits was used in the last section to establish Godel's theorem, and thus the falsity of provable determinism, the physical existence of random subatomic happenings demonstrates the untenability of determinism proper.

Some have been unwilling to accept this and have objected, as Einstein did, that "God does not throw dice," that there must be some "hidden variables" whose values, were we to know them, would lead to completely deterministic predictions. That this is logically and physically impossible is demonstrated by self-implicating questions and observations and the quantum mechanical facts. Just how extraordinary one such fact is, is clarified by an inequality due to J. S. Bell.

Bell's Inequality and Weirdness

This section will demonstrate, I hope, that one of the least problematical aspects of quantum mechanics is its probabilistic nature. More serious is the fact that it almost makes no sense. Almost. Imagine a device having three unconnected parts, as in figures 1 and 2 below. The part C in the middle has a button that, when pressed, sends out a particle to each of the detecting devices A and B. The dials on A and B can be set before the button is pressed, or even while the particles are in flight. (The distance between A and C need not equal the distance between B and C, and the dial for B can even be set after a particle arrives at A but before one arrives at B.) When the particles do arrive at A and B, a light flashes. The light, which may be red or green, flashes no matter how the dials on A and B are set, though whether it is the red or green light that flashes may depend on the dial settings. The dials are set independently of one another.

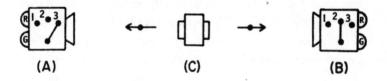

Figure 1. The complete device. *A* and *B* are the two detectors. *C* is the box from which the two particles emerge.

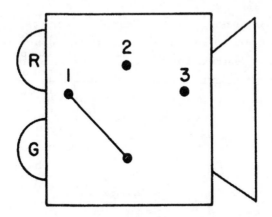

Figure 2. A detector. Particles enter on the right. The red (*R*) and green (*G*) lights are on the left. The switch is set to 1.

The nature of the particles, the construction of the device, in fact all the technical details are irrelevant. All that is important is that such a device can be built with absolutely no connections between the three parts A, B, and C. When the button is pressed, the particles are ejected and the colors of the lights on A and B are recorded. If this is repeated many times we can discern some pattern to the flashings. We indicate the outcome of any single episode by using a simple notation (due to N. David Mermin [1981], whose general approach I am following): 21RG, for example, means that A, whose dial was set at 2, flashed R while B, whose dial was set at 1, flashed G. The record of many repetitions thus would look like the following: 32RG, 21GR, 33RR, 22RR, 13RG, 32GR, 23GG, 12RG, 12GG, 11GG, 21GR, 22GG . . .

(An analogy might be helpful. Imagine two psychologists A and B in different cities, say Albuquerque and Buffalo. Married couples in Chicago separate and travel to these cities, one spouse to Albuquerque, the other to Buffalo, in order to be asked exactly one of three Yes or No questions. The psychologists' records after examining many such couples would look like the following: 31YY, 21YN, 22NN, 13NY, 11NN, 21YY, 21NY, 33YY, 21NY . . .

21YN would mean, as in the particle case, that the psychologist in Albuquerque asked question 2 and received a Yes response while the psychologist in Buffalo asked question 1 and received a No response.)

On examining this record we would notice several things: (a) When the dials on A and B have the same setting (11, 22, 33), the detectors *always* flash lights of the same color, either both red or both green. (b) For these settings, red and green pairs of flashes appear randomly with equal frequencies. (c) When the dials on A and B have different settings (12, 13, 21, 23, 31, 32), we note that the detectors flash lights of the same color only one-fourth of the time, red and green pairs of flashes appearing randomly with equal frequencies. (d) Three-quarters of the time that the dials are set differently, the lights that flash are of different colors, RG and GR appearing randomly with equal frequencies.

It is important to remember observation (c), that when the dials on A and B are set differently (12, 13, 21, 23, 31, 32), these detectors flash the same color only one-fourth of the time. Millions of trials can be run to be certain of this proportion.

Given all this, so what? Well, some strange conclusions seem forced on us. We conjecture that properties of each particle determine the color its detector will flash for each of the three dial settings. This seems to be the only way to explain why the detectors *always* flash the same color when their settings are the same: the detectors A and B must be responding to some (shared) property of the two particles— size, speed, spin, whatever.

(If, unlikely as it may seem, the members of each and every married couple were always to answer the same way, either both Yes or both No, whenever the psychologists in Albuquerque and Buffalo asked the same-numbered question, it would seem natural to conclude that the psychologists were measuring some real property of these couples.)

It would thus appear that there are eight types of parti-cles—*RRR, RRG, RGR, GRR, GGR, GRG, RGG, GGG*—and that when the dial settings are the same, the flashing of the same color on both detectors indicates the same property present for both particles. Thus if *RRG* particles are ejected by *C* and if the dials of both detectors are set at 2, the red light will flash at both *A* and *B*. If the dials are both set (indepen-dently, remember) at 3, green lights will flash at both. On the other hand, if *A*'s dial is set at 1 or 2 and *B*'s at 3, *A* will flash red and *B* green. Similarly, if *GGG* particles are eject-ed, both detectors will flash green no matter what their set-tings.

(To continue with the married couples analogy, we conclude that there are eight types of couples—*YYY, YYN, YNY, NYY, YNN, NYN, NNY, NNN*. Consider a couple of type *YNY*. If the members of this couple leave Chicago, arrive at Albuquerque and Buffalo, and are both asked question 3, they will both answer Yes. If only the Albuquerque individ-ual is asked question 3, while the Buffalo member is asked question 2, the latter will answer No while the former will still answer Yes. Similarly, if a couple of type *NYY* are asked questions 1 and 2 respectively, they will answer No and Yes respectively.)

Although he didn't consider the (analogue of the) case where the dials have different settings, Einstein concluded from a similar situation (the Einstein, Podolsky, Rosen experiment—EPR for short) that there must be "hidden variables" (the *RRG, GRG*, etc.) that determine whether the detectors will flash red or green, and that will explain why both detectors *always* flash the same color when their settings are the same. Note that in the case of the married couples this conclusion certainly seems reasonable enough.

So far, this whole discussion may seem a bit out of place and not worth pursuing (or even beginning)—something like a long shaggy-dog story without a punch line. Well, the punch line is coming. I quote from N. David Mermin's article "Quantum Mysteries for Everyone," where he writes: "The apparent inevitability of this explanation (above) for the perfect correlations when the dial settings are the same forms the basis for the conundrum posed by the device. For the explanation is quite incompatible with what happens when the dial settings are different" (1981).

Consider a particle of type *GRG*. Out of the six possible dial settings that differ (12, 21, 13, 31, 23, 32), only 13 and 31 will result in the same color flashing (green in this case). Thus for this type of particle, *GRG*, the same color should flash one-third of the time. Similarly, for particles of types *GRR, RGR, RRG, RGG*, and *GGR* the same color should flash on the detectors at *A* and *B* one-third of the time. Particles of type *RRR* or *GGG* should always flash the same color when the dial settings differ. Thus we can conclude that the only reasonable account of why the colors are always the same when the dial settings are the same implies that when the dial settings are different, the colors flashed by the detectors should be the same (at least) one-third of the time—more if there are *RRR* or *GGG* particles. But empirically this just doesn't happen: when the settings differ, the colors flashed by the detectors are the same only one-fourth of the time.

(This contrasts with what happens in the case of the married couples. Consider one such couple, say of type *YNY*. Out of the six possible question settings that differ (12, 21, 13, 31, 23, 32), only 13 and 31 will result in the same answer being given (Yes for this couple). Thus for a couple of type *YNY*, the same answer should be given one-third of the time. Similarly, for couples of types *YNN, NYN, NNY, NYY,* and *YYN* the same answer should be given in Albuquerque and Buffalo one-third of the time. Since there are also some couples of type *YYY* or *NNN*, the same answer should actually be given more than one-third of the time.)

Weirdly enough, the fraction one-fourth is what quantum mechanics predicts, contrary to the above "common-sense" estimate of at least one-third developed in a slightly different context by the physicist J. S. Bell in 1964. (In the case of the married couples, given the quite unlikely assumption that couple members always do give the same answer when asked the same question, the estimate that at least one-third of the answers will be the same when the questions differ is, as we've seen, correct.)

Realism is the commonsense philosophical view that physical objects exist independently of being perceived. It was only considered to be a philosophy of science because a case against it had been made by idealists (e.g., Berkeley in the eighteenth century), who maintained that physical objects are mind-dependent, and their being consists in being perceived. Most red-blooded scientists and philosophers are still realists, but the quantum effects exhibited in microphysical (and macrophysical) phenomena put a good deal of new stress on this position.

There is no intelligible model or mechanism that explains these phenomena, there are just certain rules for calculating and predicting probabilities (as above, $\frac{1}{4}$ instead of $\geq \frac{1}{3}$). As David Mermin writes, "The device behaves as it behaves. . . . It is not the Copenhagen interpretation of quantum mechanics that is strange, but the world itself." Physicists either become slightly mystical, postulating some quality of "wholeness" to nature (in particular to the particle pairs being measured, or to the unconnected parts A, B, and C of the device itself), or they become hardheadedly positivistic, taking refuge in their rules and formulas and abjuring intelligibility or explanatory models altogether.

Some nonphysicists (and even a few physicists) have interpreted the above experiment as indicating the existence of telepathy or instantaneous communication. The standard so-called Copenhagen interpretation of quantum mechanics rules this out, but the experimental results can nevertheless be interpreted in this way. (Even if they are, however, the "telepathy" or "instantaneous communication" involved is not of a sort that should be very comforting to these people; absolutely no message can be sent via it. The original Einstein–Podolsky–Rosen thought experiment is a simpler version of the one I've sketched here. Thus, to put it acronymically, EPR does not imply ESP.)

I wrote in the first chapter that if one understands the relevant philosophical point, one gets the joke. Not fully understanding quantum mechanics, we can't laugh quite yet (at least not heartily) at the above or other quantum mechanical puzzles. Still, I think someday we will—though, contrary to Einstein, I think that God or nature or the Great Tortoise really does throw dice.

A jest unseen, inscrutable, invisible, as a nose on a man's face.   —*William Shakespeare*

We dance round in a ring and suppose,
But the Secret sits in the middle and knows.
                                        —*Robert Frost*

"In just 38 months, you can earn BIG PROFITS as a fully trained QUANTUM MECHANIC. Learn secrets of QUANTUM MECHANICS in your own home, in your spare time, without quitting your present job! The nation is crying for fully trained QUANTUM MECHANICS.

"You get professional equipment to learn with. You will receive a professional cyclotron, actual atoms, and a year's supply of Preparation A for your

atomic piles. Only $675. Cheap when you consider
how proud you'll be to hear your son say "My
Daddy's a QUANTUM MECHANIC!"

—*anonymous, magazine parody*

On Assumptions

Risking cerebral whiplash, let me momentarily flash back 2500 years to Zeno of Elea. Zeno wrote that Achilles could never catch the turtle, since by the time Achilles had reached the place P_0 from which the turtle had started, the turtle would have advanced to P_1. When Achilles reached P_1, the turtle would have advanced to P_2; by the time Achilles had reached P_2, the turtle would have advanced to P_3; and so on. Achilles would have to cover an infinite number of such intervals before he could catch and surpass the turtle. We know now that the sum of an infinite number of (interval) lengths can be finite (e.g., $\frac{1}{2} + \frac{1}{4} + \frac{1}{8} + \frac{1}{16} + \frac{1}{32} + \ldots = 1$). Along with some theorems on infinite sets due to Georg Cantor, this knowledge resolves Zeno's paradox.

It's a reasonable conjecture that some comparable sort of conceptual advance will be necessary if we are to understand (and not just predict) quantum phenomena. The presuppositions of classical physics that will probably have to be modified concern the notion of "thinghood." What is it to be a thing? How is it that things persist through time? Are things distinct, or are they fuzzy? Are they independent, or somehow interconnected? It may very well turn out that we do not know very much about things.

The American philosopher Hilary Putnam has written that just as the development of non-Euclidean geometry made possible the easy expression of Einstein's relativity theory, so might the development of a quantum nonclassical logic make easier and more natural the expression of quantum theoretical insights about "things." The law of the excluded middle, for example, might be modified (or it might not).

Imagine a list, in some order, of all the infinitely many numbers between 0 and 10: 7.1, $2^{33}/_{49}$, π, $9^{112}/_{219}$, $5\sqrt{2}$, $\sqrt[3]{19}$, 2.86312, $\ldots$, e^2, $5^{11}/_{103}$, $\ldots$. Around the first number, place an interval of length $^1/_2$; around the second number, an interval of length $^1/_4$; around the third number, an interval of $^1/_8$; around the fourth, an interval of $^1/_{16}$, and so on. The sum of these intervals is $^1/_2 + ^1/_4 + ^1/_8 + ^1/_{16} + ^1/_{32} + \ldots = 1$, yet to most people it would seem that these intervals cover all the points on the number line between 0 and 10. What assumption are they (or you) making that Georg Cantor didn't make?

George is running up the aisle of a train traveling at 20 mph. If he's running 10 mph with respect to the train, he's moving at 30 mph with respect to the ground. It's natural to assume that velocities always add in this way—but the theory of special relativity states that this is not the case for very large velocities. Likewise, it's natural to assume that of any two space-time events, one must necessarily precede the other for all observers—but again, it isn't so.

Martha and a big dog are standing at a bus stop. Waldo approaches them and asks if her dog bites. She assures him that her dog is very friendly and doesn't bite, whereupon Waldo pets the dog. The dog bites his arms and legs and thoroughly mauls Waldo, who screams at Martha, "I though you said your dog doesn't bite!" Martha responds quite innocently, "Oh, that's not my dog."

Waldo asked his doctor how to improve his relationship with his wife. The doctor advised him to take a ten-mile walk each night so he wouldn't be so irritable, and to call him in a month. When Waldo called the next month, the doctor asked him how things were with his wife. "Fine, I'm very relaxed, but I'm three hundred miles from home!"

The moral is obvious. Suppositions, assumptions, pre-suppositions, whatever you want to call them, are necessary in order to do science or to "do" life, but they can be mis-leading and even dangerous when made unthinkingly. Unfortunately (or fortunately), they usually *must* be made unthinkingly.

Once entrenched, theories can be difficult to displace. Just as Ptolemy added epicycle to epicycle to save his theory of planetary orbit, people tend to embellish and embroider any barely serviceable theory and often even prefer such baroque theories to simpler ones.

Dr. Paul Watzlawick (1977) relates a story about a relevant piece of research due to Professor A. Bavelas: Two subjects A and B are asked to try by trial and error to recognize the difference between healthy and sick cells. They can only respond "Healthy" or "Sick" to the slides that are shown them. They are told that a light will signal when they have answered correctly. In fact, however, only A's correct responses are always greeted by the light signal. Unknown to B, who is seated across the room (and who sees the same slides in the same order), B's responses are greeted by the light signal only when A responds correctly. Whether B responds "Healthy" or "Sick" has no effect on the reinforcing light signal that he sees.

Afterward, when asked to explain their "theory of healthy cells," A's theory is simple, concrete, and straightforward. B's ideas, on the other hand, are complex, convoluted, and elaborate. Most surprisingly, A is impressed by the "brilliance" of B's theory and in a subsequent trial does considerably worse than in his first trial, presumably having been influenced by B's abstruse (Ptolemaic) ideas.

Of course, no formal research is needed to note that, everything being equal, people are often more impressed by mumbo-jumbo that they don't understand than by simple observations and deductions that they do understand. They prefer hairy hypotheses to shaving with Occam's razor.

The mathematician Howard Eves (1958) recounts the tale of a man who loved to walk. His problem was that (like Waldo earlier) he often found himself far from home at nightfall. He thus decided to buy a house on the side of a big hill and walked around the hill once each day, starting in the morning with the rising sun behind him and ending back at his house at dusk with the setting sun ahead of him. After a few years of this he discovered to his horror that his uphill leg had shortened considerably. The man then decided to walk in the other direction for a few years until he evened the length of his legs. When neighbors doubted his story, he always responded by pulling up his trousers and saying, "Look, aren't my two legs the same length?"

Needless to say, therapists ("She had such and such a depressive disorder and now she's cured"), economic forecasters, political pundits ("There was a tremendous backlash, but now attitudes toward such and such have become stable"), and the proverbial man in the street (as well as the proverbial man on the hill) are all sometimes prone to support their diagnoses and "cures" with similar arguments.

Assumptions structure one's thinking, and hence at times obstruct the seeing of certain "obvious" phenomena and ensure the seeing of certain "nonexistent" phenomena. (The quotes indicate that what is obvious or nonexistent depends to some extent on one's theoretical assumptions.)

For example, chemists before Lavoisier did not observe many of the phenomena associated with rust and oxidation, since their theoretical assumptions concerning phlogiston made it unlikely that these phenomena would be noticed. Biologists before Harvey, though they could not find any, were convinced there were holes between the left and right halves of the heart, since their theories pointed to such a conclusion.

Scientists often behave like Van Dumholtz does in the following story, though the esoteric nature of their concerns helps to keep this relatively secret:

Van Dumholtz has two large jars before him, one containing many fleas, the other empty. He gently removes a flea from the flea jar, places it on the table before the empty jar, steps back, and commands "Jump," whereupon the flea jumps into the empty jar. Methodically he gently removes each flea, places it on the table, says "Jump," and the flea jumps into the originally empty jar.

When he has transferred all the fleas in this way, he removes one from the now full jar, carefully pulls off its back legs, and places it on the table before the original jar. He commands "Jump," but the flea does not move. He takes another flea from the jar, carefully pulls off its back legs, and places it on the table. Again he commands "Jump," but the flea does not move. Methodically he goes through this same procedure with the remaining fleas, and gets the same results.

Van Dumholtz beamingly records in his notebook: "A flea when its back legs are pulled off, cannot hear."

Finally, teleological explanations make reference to the end state or purpose of some phenomenon in order to explain that phenomenon. Such explanations, for example, were (and still are) used to counter Darwin's theory of evolution. Voltairean parodies of them—rabbits have white tails so as to be more easily hunted, noses have bridges to ensure the comfortable placement of eyeglasses, etc.—are well known. Much less known is the argument advanced by Hy Marx (Groucho's great-uncle and a famous teleological physiologist) to account for the foul odor associated with flatulence: the smell, Hy explained, was for the benefit of the deaf.

In contrast, there are also legitimate uses of teleological explanation, especially if such explanations ("the thermostat is trying to keep the house at a steady temperature," e.g.) can be reformulated in nonpurposive terms or, in more complex cases, in terms of the stability of systems with interacting parts. Kant, in fact, wrote that the ability to recognize purposiveness in nature, or teleological judgment as he called it, is intimately connected with "common sense."

Another legitimate variant of teleological explanation will be discussed in the next chapter.

chapter four

PEOPLE

Context, Complexity, and Artificial Intelligence

READ: Out of Sight, Out of Mind
PRINT: Blind Idiot

Researchers in the field of artificial intelligence have been concerned with the construction of programs to translate articles from one natural language to another. Earlier workers vastly underestimated the complexity of the task, however. Something of the flavor of the problems encountered is given by the following apocryphal story: An early Russian-English, English-Russian translating program took "The spirit is willing, but the flesh is weak," translated it into Russian, and then retranslated this Russian translation back into English. The result was "The vodka is agreeable, but the meat is too tender."

Whenever there is a metaphoric component to a passage, as above, or a dependence on context or background knowledge, similar problems arise. On the other hand, if the task if formal, if there are hard-and-fast rules to follow, as in the game of chess, the performance is, of course, much more impressive. In fact it is incomparably easier for a computer to determine trajectories for space vehicles, say, than it is for it to carry on an ordinary open-ended conversation (via video screens) with a human interlocutor. The latter feat is not even close to being accomplished. If and when a computer is programmed with enough structured factual knowledge, memory, and self-modifiability to carry on such a conversation in a manner indistinguishable from that of another person, it will have passed (Alan) Turing's test for machine intelligence.

To pass the Turing test, not only must an awesome amount of informal and mundane knowledge be formalized (mustard is not put on bananas or in one's shoes, cats do not grow on trees, raincoats are not made out of rain) but differences in significance due to context must also somehow be provided for. How, to cite a common example, is a computer to evaluate a remark about a man touching his head without knowing the context in which it occurs? It could mean indefinitely many things, depending on indefinitely many ever-changing human contexts. Even if enough knowledge of the most likely contexts is programmed in, it is commonly the case in conversation that the context of a term is supplied only within the bit of dialogue in which it appears. A specific example is provided by the following story, but this openness and sensitivity to context, this being-thereness, is pervasive.

A young man on vacation calls home and speaks to his brother. "How's Oscar the cat?"

"The cat's dead, died this morning."

"That's terrible. You know how attached I was to him. Couldn't you have broken the news more gently?"

"How?"

"You could've said that he's on the roof. Then the next

time I called you could have said that you haven't been able to get him down, and gradually like this you could've broken the news."

"Okay, I see. Sorry."

"Anyway, how's Mom?"

"She's on the roof."

The dog moves his rook to KB4 with his paw. George moves his queen to QB6 and announces, "Checkmate. That was a stupid move, dog. Besides having bad breath, you're really dumb. I've beaten you five out of seven games."

There is an interesting tendency that workers in artificial intelligence (the least critical, most gung-ho of whom are sometimes castigated as members of the "artificial intelligentsia" by disgruntled art historians) often complain about: Any activity or task—such as translating novel passages from one natural language to another—that is resistant to performance by a computer is defined as requiring "real" intelligence. Conversely, anytime a program is written that accomplishes some task or other, such as the many chess-playing programs, many people dismiss the task as not requiring real intelligence. This tendency to dismiss as not really constitutive of intelligence those activities formalized enough to be captured by a program should not, I think, be considered an after-the-fact redefinition of intelligence, but rather a reevaluation of the various kinds of intelligence.

Performing many different tasks, using many different procedures, determining when one rather than another is appropriate, discovering the limits of a method's applicability, modifying a system to adapt to different circumstances—these activities are all of a different order of difficulty and require a more flexible sort of integrative intelligence than does working within a well-defined formal system such as chess or celestial mechanics. Necessary in order for this "integrative intelligence" to function in putting together the disparate and incongruous details of an informal situation and making them coherent is a personality of sorts—wants, interests, a sense of self.

It is tempting to speculate that the high-status jobs of the future will be those that place a premium on these self-mediated integrative activities, rather than on any particular formalized skill. Generally, the more interesting and important a job, the less well-defined it is. Housewives and househusbands, handymen, humorists, philosophers, good conversationalists, friends, and lovers—all may be valued even more highly in the future than they are today.

Marvin Minsky, an eminent computer scientist, has written, "When intelligent machines are constructed, we should not be surprised to find them as confused and as stubborn as men on their convictions about mind-matter, consciousness, free will, and the like." This seems to make some sense, though I would substitute an "if" for the "when" above.

In addition to philosophical concerns, these intelligent "machines" will probably have a sense of humor. In fact, a variation of the Turing test for machine intelligence would be to construct a program that recognizes jokes. All the intellectual integrative skills mentioned earlier would be required, along with an appreciation of emotional nuance. This combination of skills is not so common, come to think of it, even among humans.

A very old married couple in their nineties visit a divorce lawyer. He asks, "Why now? You're both in your nineties, you've been married for more than seventy years, why get divorced now?"

They explain, "We wanted to wait until the children were dead."

If you chuckled, you probably don't have silicon in your brain (steel in your heart maybe, but not silicon in your brain).

It's conceivable that with the advance of artificial intelligence, ethnic jokes will be replaced by robot jokes:

Two robot bear hunters were driving along when they came upon a sign that said "Bear Left," whereupon they returned home.

The robot pharmacist quit his job. He couldn't fit the little prescription bottles into the typewriter.

An important distinction in computer science is that between the hardware and the software of the computer. Although the distinction is not always clear-cut, "hardware" refers to the physical aspects of the computer (tapes, disks, transistors, chips, etc.), whereas "software" refers to the programs that run on the computer. The program determines what the computer does, what the sequence of logical or programmatic states must be. Corresponding to these logical or programmatic states of the computer are the physical states of its hardware.

Hilary Putnam has noted that the logical and linguistic questions and issues that arise concerning this software-hardware distinction are similar in some important respects to those arising in the traditional mind-body problem of Descartes. What is the relationship between mind and brain (body)? How does one affect the other? Are the mental and physical incommensurable, or are they different aspects of the same phenomenon? These problems, Putnam claims, have in some respects solutions (or dissolutions) identical to those of the following analogous problems: What is the relationship between program and hardware? How does one affect the other? Are programmatic and hardware properties incommensurable, or different aspects of the same phenomenon?

Compare:

(1) I want George to cry at this point in the play, so while he's backstage either have him think of something very sad or, if he can't, drip onion juice into his eyes.

(2) I want that strange helical pattern to appear on the monitor at this point in the presentation, so either program its appearance or, if you can't, rub a magnet over the interface cable like this.

The topic of the next section (intensional explanations) sheds a little light on some related questions.

Why Did He Just Now Touch His Head?

"And the problem arises: what is left over if I subtract the fact that my arm goes up from the fact that I raise my arm?"

—*Ludwig Wittgenstein*

MYRTLE: Why do you think that man over there just touched his head?

GEORGE: He's the third-base coach and he's giving the bunt signal to the batter.

MARTHA: It's a windy day and he's making sure his hairpiece is snug.

WALDO: A complex set of neuron firings and muscle contractions brought about by an even more complex set of chemical and physical phenomena caused the upper right appendage to move at such and such an angle and rate of speed to the lateral part of the uppermost central extremity.

MYRTLE: Huh?

The explanations of George and Martha differ from Waldo's in a crucial way: they explain by giving a reason for the behavior in question, rather than by citing causal laws. By giving a rationale for the behavior, George and Martha make it reasonable in light of certain socially accepted rules and norms, and the beliefs and intentions of the agent. Explanations of this type, which presuppose the rationality of the agents involved, are called intensional explanations. Waldo's explanation, on the other hand, is a causal one: If these general covering laws are valid, and if these conditions obtain, then that will result.

Note that there is no conflict between the two types of explanation. Both types can be invoked to explain the same bit of behavior (Princess Diana's becoming pregnant, the Watergate tapes being erased), though one or the other may be more appropriate in any given context.

It's interesting that Freud, who started out as a "hard" scientist, attempted in his "Scientific Project" to reconcile causal (neurophysiological) explanation and intensional (psychoanalytic in this case) explanation. He wrote that he wanted "to furnish a psychology that shall be a natural science: that is, to represent psychical processes as quantitatively determinate states of specifiable material particles, thus making those processes perspicuous and free from contradiction" (1966). He failed, of course, since his neurological knowledge was limited, his psychoanalytic theories were flawed (to be kind), and the connection, even between two ideal approaches, was and is almost unimaginably complex.

Even in purely physical contexts, intensional explanations may sometimes be the only manageable ones. Playing chess with a computer, for example, requires that one adopt what Daniel Dennett (1978) calls an "intentional stance" toward it rather than a physical one. One predicts (and explains) the computer's moves by asking oneself what is the most rational move given the goal of the program (winning), the constraints on it (the rules of chess), its store of information (perfect memory of all past moves), and its "personality" as so far revealed (tendency to castle, move its queen, and so on). One does not try to predict or explain the computer's moves by examining the physical state of its circuits, chips, and disks, because to do so is again much, much too difficult, and prohibitively time-consuming.

The notion of an action is useful in clarifying the relation between intensional and causal explanations. An action is a bit of behavior for which the agent's reasons are the cause. The erratic movement of an epileptic is not an action, nor is the backward fall of a man sitting on a rickety chair that collapses suddenly; a causal explanation is most appropriate in these cases. On the other hand, jumping around energetically to alert an airplane overhead and a backward double somersault, though they resemble the previous behaviors, are both actions. It should be clear also from the example of a man touching his head that a bit of behavior can be seen as indefinitely many different actions depending on the person, his background, the immediate context of the behavior, and the general culture. The man might have touched his head in the belief that he would thus appear relaxed and unconcerned while his neighbors discussed a local burglary, a burglary the man himself committed. Causal explanations do not have the variety and dependence on context that intensional explanations do.

Though the reasons of an action are its cause, it is important to remember that they cannot be determined except in the context of an intensional explanation. One first determines what action a person is performing, why it is rational, and then identifies that person's reasons as the cause of the action.

My son often fights with my daughter, and sometimes in defense he explains, "I didn't punch her. My arm was just moving and her face was in the way."

The French writer Henri Bergson attributed laughter to the "mechanical encrusted on something living" (1911). By this rather celebrated phrase he meant that a person who becomes rigid, machinelike, and repetitive becomes laughable, since the essence of humanity is its (relative) flexibility and spirit. "Any incident is comic that calls our attention to the physical in a person when it is the moral side that is concerned. . . . We laugh everytime a person gives the impression of being a thing" (1911). Slipping, falling, digesting, twitching—none of these are actions, none admit of intentional explanations, and all, in a suitable context, are funny.

Hamlet hiccoughs, the president burps, or the mob boss slips on a banana peel, and we laugh. On a somewhat higher level, philosophers (which most people are, to some extent) laugh when someone makes a category mistake of some sort. Philosophy is devoted to the never-ending task of seeing beyond the "mechanical encrustations" on our understanding.

GEORGE: This talk of intentional explanations is sloppy. Why don't we use only causal explanations?

MARTHA: You're right. Let's just *decide* right now to do that. We both *want* to clarify, and causal explanations seem clearer and more precise.

The joke, such as it is, is that Martha is offering an intentional explanation of why she and George are planning to use only causal explanations. Intentional notions are built into the fabric of our communication. The American philosopher H. P. Grice has even analyzed "*S*'s meaning something by *x*" as "*S*'s intending the utterance of *x* to produce some effect in a hearer by means of the hearer's recognition of *S*'s intention to produce that effect" (1957). For practical purposes, causal explanation correlates of intentional explanations are quite useless.

An important way in which the logic of intentional explanations differs from that of causal ones is in the failure of extensionality. That is, the substitution of an expression referring to a person or thing for another expression referring to that same person or thing can change the truth-value of intentional statements and the cogency of intentional explanations. This is not the case for causal statements or explanations. For example, consider again George's explanation of why the man was touching his head. (He's the third-base coach and he's giving the bunt signal to the batter.) Suppose that the third-base coach is Henry Malone's cousin and the batter is the only Greek on the field. Upon substitution of these expressions, the "explanation" of the man's touching his head becomes "He's Henry Malone's cousin and he's giving the bunt signal to the Greek." One could even replace "giving the bunt signal to" with "stroking his temple for," an expression referring to the same movement, and lose all explanatory power. The substitution of an expression having the same referent for an expression in Waldo's causal explanation—say, by using a different coordinate system, or a different description of "upper right appendage"—does not affect the truth-value of any statement, or the explanatory power of the explanation. Thus in intentional, but not in causal, explanations, how a person or thing is referred to or described is important. Even though Oedipus wanted to marry Jocasta, Jocasta was his mother, and presumably Oedipus did not want to marry his mother.

A confusion or conflation of subject and object always results in undecidable, open questions. Recall the brilliant computer whose yes-no device turned the attached light-bulb off and on. The subject-object conflation resulted in the undecidability by the machine of certain questions involving the lightbulb.

More commonly one forms a model of a situation, and if one is a part of that situation, one objectifies that part of oneself so involved. The account of the situation is then necessarily incomplete, however, since a part of the subject-observer is always doing the observing and that part is not being self-observed. This logical problem represents a "problem," of course, only when one wants a "complete" account or explanation of something, when one becomes too greedy a scientist. There's no problem if one is simply dancing or fighting, making love or practicing Zen, picking grapes or picking one's nose.

Intentional explanations in general involve such sub-ject-object blurs, since they require of one enough empathy to understand the rules, values, and beliefs of another person whose responses and actions are in turn thereby affect-ed. Compare Grice's account of communication above. Except in the case of quantum phenomena (Heisenberg uncertainty principle), causal explanations generally don't have this property. A rock is not affected by any calculations or explanations of its trajectory, for example.

GEORGE: Hi, Martha.

MARTHA: What's the matter, George? Are you mad at me?

GEORGE: No, of course not.

MARTHA: Yes you are. Why are you mad?

GEORGE: I'm not, I told you.

MARTHA: You are. I can tell by the tone of your voice.

GEORGE: Martha, I am trying not to be angry with you.

MARTHA: See, you're seething with hostility toward me.
Why? What did I ever do to deserve such anger?

George stalks away, slamming the door behind him.

The *National Inquirer*, a strange yet intriguing gossip-filled tabloid of news and pseudo-news, often carries stories about why show-business celebrities X and Y are in love. The stories, I would guess, often play a role in the subsequent appearance of stories about why celebrities X and Y are now involved with Z and W, respectively. Even "neutral, objective" observation of people often significantly affects their behavior; consider surveys of the frequency of various sexual practices, for example. However, people sometimes overestimate the effect that their doings will have on others. Such may be the case with the confused statistician in the following story:

Howard Eves (1958) tells about a statistician who traveled widely giving lectures. He was, however, apprehensive about flying, especially since there had been some recent bomb scares aboard airplanes. He calculated the probability of a bomb being aboard a plane and was reassured that it was reasonably small. Then he calculated the probability of there being two bombs aboard a plane and found it to be absolutely infinitesimal. Hence he always traveled with a bomb in his suitcase.

Intentional explanations are probabilistic for several reasons. First is the subject-object blur just discussed. Explaining, even observing, often changes what is explained or observed, certainly with respect to oneself and those close to oneself. The second reason is the nature and level of the explanation. Providing a plausible, broad-scale rationale for an action is not the same as providing a set of sufficient causal conditions for it. A (or many) rationale(s) for a potential action is (are) never sufficient to ensure that the action will take place. No matter how many cogent reasons there are to do something, a person (or other intelligence) may still decide not to do it.

Microphysical indeterminism may, as I've already noted, be a third source for the probabilistic nature of intentional explanations. It is conceivable that this quantum indeterminism is somehow filtered through the structured complexity of the mind-brain, resulting in the possibility of metaphysically free action. (Bertrand Russell once speculated, "It might be that without infringing the laws of physics, intelligence could make improbable things happen, as Maxwell's demon would have defeated the second law of thermodynamics by opening the trap door to fast-moving particles and closing it to slow-moving particles.") Ideas (some unconscious) might be generated in part by an indeterministic process, the viable ones surviving the tests of reality and consciousness. The similarity to biological natural selection is especially appealing. In any case, this third source is not required, as even intentional explanations or predictions of the moves of fully determined chess-playing computers are still, practically speaking, only probabilistic.

Finally, it should not be assumed that the value of an explanation is measured by how probable its conclusion is, as George shows Waldo:

WALDO: The value of an explanation is only as good as the probability of its conclusion.

GEORGE: What am I doing?

WALDO: It looks like you're rolling a pair of dice.

GEORGE: You're right. I just rolled a seven. Why?

WALDO: Chance. One-sixth of the time you'll roll a seven, that's all.

GEORGE: Now I've rolled a twelve. Why?

WALDO: Chance again. One-thirty-sixth of the time you'll roll a twelve.

GEORGE: The explanations seem to be the same even though the probabilities of their conclusions differ.

In intentional explanations as well as causal ones, a low probability for the conclusion does not necessarily mean a poor explanation. Our specific, personal genetic makeup, for example, is an improbable accident: a different sperm might have united with the same or a different egg and we wouldn't have been. Still, the explanation for our personal genetic makeup depends on the particular sperm and egg that did, however improbably, unite.

Arrow, Prisoners, and Compromise

A young boy is quietly masturbating in his room when his mother walks in. "Don't do that, son, or you'll go blind."
"Mom, couldn't I do it just until I need glasses?"

Two dangers threaten the world—order and disorder.

—*Paul Valéry*

Moderation has been recognized as a virtue since the time of the Greeks. The problem with the injunction "Be moderate," however, is that it's almost meaningless without some standard scale against which to measure oneself and one's actions. Even in elementary mathematics, "Be moderate" faces difficulties. If the side of a cube ranges between 0 and 2 inches, then, assuming we know nothing else of the distribution of cube sizes, the average cube might be said to have a side of 1 inch. Yet if instead we consider the volumes of these cubes, which must range between 0 and 8 cubic inches, we might say that the average cube has a volume of 4 cubic inches. Thus, using two different standards, the "average" cube has a side of 1 inch and a volume of 4 cubic inches.

Late in the eighteenth century Jeremy Bentham tried to develop a "hedonic calculus" that would measure the utilities and disutilities of an action. With the aid of such a tool we could "act so as to maximize the net amount of utility" (1948). How then does this wonderful calculus measure utilities and disutilities, or, more plainly, pleasure and pains? Unfortunately (or more likely, fortunately), it doesn't exist. Bentham and others since him have failed to find any reasonable way to add up the incommensurables of human life. (There is no trick in finding unreasonable or arbitrary ways, or even reasonable ways in narrow contexts.)

Though Bentham said little about how to compare the utility of disparate qualities—beauty vs. intelligence, wealth vs. health—he did suggest that for any one quality, "extent," "duration," and "intensity" were reasonable dimensions to consider. They are, of course; but problems remain. How does one measure even these dimensions of a quality? For what duration, for example, does a conversation with a friend afford one happiness—a half-hour, a week, a lifetime? How are the values of these dimensions related to the quality in question? What is the relation between the number of jokes, say, and the humorousness of a book? How do these dimensions interact with each other and with other more subtle dimensions of a quality? Can interpersonal comparisons of intensity be made? Does it make sense to say that George loves his son more than Martha loves her husband? In short, not only is there no way to compare apples with oranges, there is not even an all-purpose way to grade apples.

Still, there are *special-purpose* ways of grading apples— weight, sugar content, skin thickness, number of worms, and so on. Likewise, there are special-purpose ways of grading beauty (hair color, skin oiliness, size of ears, and so on), intelligence (special intuition, vocabulary, memory, and so on), health (weight, various blood counts, number of operations, and so on). As long as these special-purpose orderings and rankings are recognized as rough, circumstantial, and conditional, much of the crassness of such rankings can be avoided.

MARTHA: Is he smart?

MYRTLE: Yeah, his IQ is 160.

MARTHA: Is he rich?

MYRTLE: He makes $400,000 a year.

MARTHA: Is he good-looking?

MYRTLE: He makes Paul Newman look like Rodney Dangerfield.

MARTHA: Is he friendly, sexy?

MYRTLE: Everyone knows him. He's always at some party or other, girls draped all over him.

MARTHA: Do you like him?

MYRTLE: I can't stomach the sight of him. He's plastic, phony, and insensitive. Just hearing his voice makes my flesh crawl.

GEORGE: Sure is hot today, about 80° I'd say.

WALDO: Yeah, got down to 40° last night. It's twice as hot now.

On the subject of hot summer days, there was a midwestern state legislator who opposed the adoption of daylight savings time because the increased daylight would more quickly fade curtains and fabrics.

That balance and moderation, a sense of perspective, and the harmonious integration of disparate elements are valued is evidenced by the laughter occasioned by their absence. Exaggeration and distortion, in particular, often lead to humor. The following is an old story due to George Bernard Shaw. It seems more appropriate with Groucho, however:

GROUCHO (*to woman seated next to him at an elegant dinner party*): Would you sleep with me for ten million dollars?

WOMAN (*giggling*): Oh, Groucho, of course I would.

GROUCHO: How about doing it for fifteen dollars?

WOMAN (*indignant*): Why, what do you think I am?

GROUCHO: That's already been established. Now we're just haggling about the price.

Politics is the art of balance and compromise. Consider the fact that the two most important ideals—liberty and equality—are, in their purest form, incompatible: complete liberty results in inequality, while enforced equality results in loss of liberty. Liberty and equality must thus be balanced, refined, made conditional. The differences between the political right and the political left can be simplistically described as a difference between prepositions, between freedom *to* (speak, move about, buy and sell, etc.) and freedom *from* (hunger, joblessness, etc.). The following pair of stories point up a couple of these differences:

George and Waldo come upon a couple of apples, one large, the other small. George, being quicker, grabs the larger apple and gobbles it up, while Waldo just manages to get hold of the smaller one.

WALDO: "That's not polite, George. If I'd reached here first, I would have left the larger apple for you."

GEORGE: "Then what are you complaining about? You got what you wanted."

George, Martha, Waldo, and Myrtle come upon a loaf of bread. They decide to divide it evenly, and use the following procedure: George cuts off what he considers to be a quarter of the loaf. If Martha thinks the piece is a quarter of the loaf or less, she doesn't touch it; if she thinks it's bigger than a quarter of the loaf, she cuts off a sliver to make it exactly a quarter. Waldo then either leaves the piece alone or trims it further if he thinks it's still bigger than a quarter of the loaf. Finally, Myrtle has the same option: trim it if it's too big, or leave it alone if it's not. The last person to touch the slice keeps it. This finished, there are three people remaining who must divide the rest of the cake evenly. The same procedure is followed: the first person cuts off what he considers to be a third of the remaining loaf, and so on. In this way everyone is satisfied that he or she has received a quarter of the loaf.

The following story is due to Raymond Smullyan (1980):

GEORGE: Mmm, chocolate cake. I'm going to eat all of it.

MARTHA: I want dessert, too. We should split it 50-50.

GEORGE: I want all of it.

MARTHA: No, we have to split it evenly. Let's ask Myrtle to decide. She's always fair.

MYRTLE: You should compromise: three-fourths for George, and one-fourth for you, Martha.

Mort Sahl remarked that in the 1980 election many people did not vote for Ronald Reagan so much as they voted against Jimmy Carter. He continued, "If Reagan had been unopposed, he would've lost."

People have individual preferences out of which, since these preferences often differ, group preferences must be fashioned. This is obviously a difficult practical problem. It is a more difficult theoretical problem, in a certain sense even an impossible one.

Consider first a voting paradox due to the eighteenth-century French philosopher Condorcet. Three candidates—

George, Martha, and Waldo—are running for governor of Wisconowa. A third of the electorate prefers George to Martha to Waldo; another third of the electorate prefers Martha to Waldo to George; and the remaining third prefers Waldo to George to Martha. There is nothing especially unusual about this unless we consider what happens in two-person races given the above preferences. George can boast that two-thirds of the electorate prefers him to Martha. Waldo responds that two-thirds of the electorate prefers him to George. Finally, Martha counters by noting that two-thirds of the electorate prefers her to Waldo.

If the societal preferences in this example are determined by majority vote, we have an irrational societal ordering of preferences—that is, "society" prefers George over Martha, Martha over Waldo, and Waldo over George. Thus even if the preferences of all the individual voters are transitive (transitivity holds if, whenever a voter prefers x to y and y to z, he or she prefers x to z), the societal preferences determined by majority vote are not necessarily transitive (rational).

A general theorem can be proved showing that all "reasonable" voting systems (or equivalently, economic market systems) are subject to such irrationalities; but before discussing this, it should be pointed out that individuals are not immune to Condorcet's paradox.

The mathematician Paul Halmos has proposed the following variation of the paradox that applies to individuals: Imagine a woman trying to decide which of three cars to buy: Car G, Car M, or Car W. She, being a methodical sort, had three criteria (of equal weight) for making this decision: looks, affordability, and performance. Car G looked better than Car M, which looked better than Car W. On the other hand, Car M was more affordable than Car W, which in turn was more affordable than Car G. Finally, Car W performed better than Car G, which performed better than Car M. Since the woman placed equal weight on each of these criteria, she was in a quandary. She clearly preferred Car G to Car M (G outscored M on two criteria). She also preferred Car M to Car W (for the same reason). Yet she preferred Car W to Car G.

Though the same problem of nontransitivity holds for individuals, it seems somehow more tractable. In the case above you just have to induce the woman to declare one of the criteria more important than the others. This is easier than convincing one-third of an electorate to change its mind.

The economist Kenneth J. Arrow proved (1951) an interesting generalization of Condorcet's paradox. He showed that there is no way to derive societal or group preferences from individual preferences that can be guaranteed to satisfy the following four minimal conditions: The societal preferences (1) must be transitive (if society prefers x to y and y to z, then it must prefer x to z); (2) must satisfy the Pareto principle (if alternative x is preferred to alternative y by everyone in the society, then society must prefer x to y); (3) must satisfy the independence of irrelevant alternatives (the societal preference depends only on the orderings of the individuals with respect to alternatives *in* that environment); and (4) must not be susceptible to dictatorship (there is no individual whose preferences automatically determine all of society's preferences).

COMMUNIST: "Man's inhumanity to man," that is what capitalism is all about.

GEORGE: Yes, in communism it is the other way around.

Bumper sticker: GOD SAID IT, I BELIEVE IT, AND THAT SETTLE'S IT. (The apostrophe is most informative.)

There was once a scorpion who wanted to cross a river. Spotting a turtle on a rock, the scorpion asked if he would take him across the river. In return he would show the turtle where he could find some very succulent vegetation.

The turtle responded, "How can I be sure you won't sting my neck?"

"Don't be silly," the scorpion replied. "If I did that, we'd both drown."

The turtle was convinced, and they began swimming toward the vegetation the scorpion had told him about. When they had nearly reached the far side of the river, however, the scorpion stung him in the neck after all. Struggling to make it to the river bank, the turtle gasped,

"Why, why did you do this to me?"

Hopping off the dying turtle's back, the scorpion explained, "I thought you might dive under the water to drown me."

The Prisoners' Dilemma is another old puzzle with societal implications. Imagine two prisoners Waldo and George against whom there is little real evidence. Although these prisoners have committed a crime, they can expect little punishment (say one year in prison) if they both remain silent. If George confesses to their crime, however, and Waldo remains silent, George will be released while Waldo can expect a five-year sentence. Conversely, if Waldo talks and George remains silent, Waldo will be released while George can expect a five-year sentence. Thus each man has a choice of confessing or not. If they both confess, each gets a three-year term; if they're both silent, each gets a one-year term; if A confesses and B is silent, A gets off and B gets five years.

The punchline, so to speak, is that the optimum course of action, remaining silent, is in general not the course that George and Waldo are likely to follow: they're both likely to confess so as to avoid being a patsy for the other. This situation is, of course, not limited to prisoners. Spouses in a marriage, businessmen in a competitive market, and national governments in an arms race can all fall subject to such prisoners' dilemmas. Adam Smith's invisible hand ensuring that individual pursuits will necessarily ensure group well-being is at times quite arthritic.

Results like Arrow's paradox and the Prisoners' Dilemma, the well-known problems of quantification and measurement in the social sciences (6.28 on the pleasure scale, 2.89 on the pain scale, let's do it), and the inherent riskiness of all explanation, especially intentional explanation, should, but probably won't, make for cautious skepticism in predicting ourselves, society, and the future. Lewis Carroll's Cheshire Cat reminds us of the single most important, yet unpredictable, determinant of that future:

"Would you tell me please, which way I ought to go from here," asked Alice.

"That depends a good deal on where you want to get to," said the Cat.

AFTERWORD

> When I was young, I forgot to laugh. Later when I opened my eyes and saw reality I began to laugh and haven't stopped since.   —*Soren Kierkegaard*

Wittgenstein once remarked that he looked forward to the day when philosophy was no longer a subject in its own right but rather infused all other subjects. Philosophy is (or should be), in this view, an adverb: one does linguistics philosophically, one studies science philosophically, one investigates political issues philosophically. Humor or play has something of the same character. It's awkward for humor itself to be the focus of an activity. The announcement "We will now tell jokes and be humorous" sounds distinctly totalitarian. Humor too is adverbial and qualifies one's approach to other activities: one answers questions humorously, analyzes a situation humorously, writes or speaks humorously.

Of course, "quickly," "painfully," and "odoriferously" are also adverbs, but I hope I've managed to indicate that "philosophically" and "humorously," at least in their best manifestations, share more than adverbial status. Both require a free intelligence in a relatively open society, and both evince a keen concern for language and its (mis)interpretation, as well as a skeptical tendency toward debunking. The incongruity that lies at the heart of most jokes is analogous to the conundrum that lies at the heart of most philosophical problems. Likewise, the aggressive tone present in many jokes and the social control that the jokes tend to foster are analogous to the argumentative nature of many philosophical papers and the intellectual dominance that the papers are meant to establish. It should be noted, though, that this aggressive tone and argumentative nature are clearly circumscribed and presuppose an independent intelligence in others.

Finally, both humor and philosophy are quintessentially human, requiring as they do the characteristically human ability to transcend one's self and one's situation. The discrepancy between our hopes or pretensions and reality is, try though we sometimes do, impossible not to see. Two responses to the starkness of this discrepancy are through philosophy and humor. I think, therefore I laugh.

Our heroes—Ludwig Wittgenstein, Bertrand Russell, Lewis Carroll, and Groucho Marx—are discussing the question "What is philosophy?" Let us join them for the end of their discussion and ours.

WITTGENSTEIN: I repeat, the question is not well posed. There are a whole family of uses for the term "philosophy." Still, my primary aim has been to clarify, to show how to pass from a piece of disguised nonsense to something that is obvious nonsense. Misunderstandings, as I've always insisted, must be cured if we are to be free of them.

GROUCHO: Is that anything like curing hams?

RUSSELL: Asking the question indicates, I think, that you know quite well what Mr. Wittgenstein is talking about.

GROUCHO: Easy on the self-reference shtick, Bertie. We're

not in the elevator anymore. I understand Ludwig's point, but most of this other philosophical stuff you guys dream up seems so nit-picking and technical. What about the big questions: the meaning of life, the death of God, the residuals on my television reruns?

RUSSELL: Better some real progress on the meaning of confirmation and probability, on the nature of logic and scientific law, on reductionism, artificial intelligence, and intentional explanation, for example, than a lot of empty blather on the so-called big questions. The big questions, at least the ones that make sense, will always be there. They're sometimes clarified by the answers to the smaller questions, sometimes not. When they're not, though, listening to woolly-headed pontificators expound on them doesn't help either. A courageous acknowledgment of ignorance is much preferable.

GROUCHO: Calm down, Bertie. Without those woolly-headed pontificators we might both be unemployed or, worse yet, lawyers. Maybe what I'm trying to get at—or be cured of, as Ludwig might say—is what difference does it all make? What difference will the answers to these smaller questions, or anything else for that matter, make in fifty thousand years? Even my reruns won't be on then, and there'll be no more copies of *Principia Mathematica*, Ludwig's *Philosophical Investigations*, or even *Alice in Wonderland*.

LEWIS CARROLL (OVERCOMING HIS SHYNESS, STAMMERS): Maybe n-n-nothing we do now will make a difference in fifty thousand years, but *if* that is so, then it would seem that nothing that will be the case in fifty thousand years makes a difference *now*, either. In particular, it doesn't make a difference now that in fifty thousand years what we do now won't make a difference.

GROUCHO: You can bet your walrus that I'm not going to tangle with you about time. The time has passed, in fact, to talk of many things. Enough. If you fellas will excuse me, I'm going to be leaving in a minute. If you persist with this talk, though, I might leave in a huff, or maybe even in a minute and a huff. In any case, since you haven't asked, I'm going over to make love with our old friend Martha. Fortunately her husband George is out looking for grue emeralds with Waldo.

Groucho slouches off, leaving the three philosophers wondering.

BIBLIOGRAPHY

Anobile, Robert J., ed. 1971. *Why a Duck*. New York: Darien House.

Arrow, K. J. 1951. *Social Choice and Individual Values*. New York: Wiley.

Barker, Stephen. 1964. *Philosophy of Mathematics*. Englewood Cliffs, N.J.: Prentice-Hall.

Bateson, Gregory. 1958. The Message "This Is Play." In B. Schaffner, ed., *Group Processes: Transactions of the Second Conference*. New York: Josiah Macy Jr. Foundation.

Bell, J. S. 1964. *Physics*.

Bentham, Jeremy. 1948. *An Introduction to the Principles of Morals and Legislation*. New York: Hafner.

Bergson, Henri. 1911. *Laughter: An Essay on the Meaning of the Comic*. New York: Macmillan.

Bohm, D. 1951. *Quantum Theory*. Englewood Cliffs, N.J.: Prentice-Hall.

Brody, Baruch. 1970. *Readings in the Philosophy of Science*. Englewood Cliffs, N.J.: Prentice-Hall.

Carroll, Lewis. 1946. *Alice's Adventures in Wonderland* and *Through the Looking Glass*. New York: Grosset and Dunlap.

Chaitin, Gregory. 1965. Randomness and Mathematical Proof. *Scientific American*, March.

Chaitin, Gregory. 1966. Complexity Theory. *Communications of the ACM*, August.

Davidson, Donald. 1963. Actions, Reasons, and Causes. *Journal of Philosophy* 60.

Dawkins, Richard. 1976. *The Selfish Gene*. New York: Oxford University Press.

DeLong, Howard. 1970. *A Profile of Mathematical Logic*. Reading, Mass.: Addison-Wesley.

Dennett, Daniel. 1978. *Brainstorms*. Vermont: Bradford Books.

Descartes, René. 1977. Meditations on First Philosophy. In *Classics of Western Philosophy*. Indianapolis: Hackett.

Dretske, Fred. 1971. Conclusive Reason. *Australasian Journal of Philosophy* 49.

Enderton, Herbert. 1972. *A Mathematical Introduction to Logic*. New York: Academic Press.

Eves, Howard. 1958. *Mathematical Circles Adieu*.

Farzan, Massud. 1973. *Another Way of Laughter*. New York: E. P. Dutton.

Frege, Gotlob. 1949. On Sense and Nominatum. In Herbert Feigl and Wilfrid Sellars, eds., *Readings in Philosophical Analysis*. New York: Appleton-Century-Crofts.

Freud, Sigmund. 1966. Project for a Scientific Psychology. In *The Standard Edition of the Complete Psychological Works of Sigmund Freud*. London: Hogarth Press and Institute for Psychoanalysis.

Fry, W. F. 1963. *Sweet Madness: A Study of Humor*. Palo Alto, Calif.: Pacific Press.

Gardner, Martin. 1973. Mathematical Games. *Scientific American*, July.

Gardner, Martin. 1981. *Gotcha*. San Francisco: Freeman Press.

Gettier, Edmund L. 1963. Is Justified True Belief Knowledge? *Analysis* 23.

Goodman, Nelson. 1965. *Fact, Fiction, and Forecast*. New York: Bobbs-Merrill.

Grice, H. P. 1957. Meaning. *Philosophical Review*.

Hempel, Carl. 1965. *Aspects of Scientific Explanation*. New York: Free Press.

Hofstadter, Douglas. 1982 and 1983. Metamagical Themas Column. *Scientific American*, January issues.

Hume, David. 1977. An Inquiry Concerning Human Understanding. In *Classics of Western Philosophy*. Indianapolis: Hackett.

Kant, Immanuel. 1977. Prolegomena to Any Future Metaphysics. In *Classics of Western Philosophy*. Indianapolis: Hackett.

Kripke, Saul. 1975. Outline of a Theory of Truth. *Journal of Philosophy*.

MacKay, D. M. 1964. Brain and Will. In *Body and Mind*. London: Allen and Unwin.

Malcolm, N. 1958. *Ludwig Wittgenstein: A Memoir*. London: Oxford University Press.

Margolis, Joseph. 1978. *An Introduction to Philosophical Inquiry*. New York: Knopf.

Mermin, N. David. 1981. Quantum Mysteries for Anyone. *Journal of Philosophy*.

Monk, Ray. 1983. *Ludwig Wittgenstein: Duty of Genius*. New York: Penguin.

Nozick, Robert. 1981. *Philosophical Explanations*. Cambridge, Mass.: Harvard University Press.

Nozick, Robert. Newcombe's Problem and Two Principles of Choice. In *Essays in Honor of Carl G. Hempel*. Dordrecht: Reidel.

Pagels, Heinz R. 1982. *The Cosmic Code*. New York: Simon and Schuster.

Pascal, Blaise. 1966. *Pensées*. London: Penguin Books.

Paulos, John A. 1980. *Mathematics and Humor*. Chicago: University of Chicago Press.

Pitcher, George. 1966. Wittgenstein, Nonsense, and Lewis Carroll. *Massachusetts Review*.

Poincaré, Henri. 1913. *The Foundations of Science*. New York: Science Press.

Popper, Karl. 1959. *The Logic of Scientific Discovery*. London: Hutchinson.

Popper, Karl. 1972. *Objective Knowledge*. Oxford: Oxford University Press.

Putnam, Hilary. 1975a. The Logic of Quantum Mechanics. In *Mathematics, Matter and Method*. Cambridge: Cambridge University Press.

Putnam, Hilary. 1975b. Minds and Machines. In *Mind, Language and Reality*. Cambridge: Cambridge University Press.

Quine, W. V. O. 1953. Two Dogmas of Empiricism. In *From a Logical Point of View*. Cambridge, Mass.: Harvard University Press.

Quine, W. V. O. 1960. *Word and Object*. Cambridge, Mass.: MIT Press.

Reichenbach, Hans. 1949. On the Justification of Induction. In Herbert Feigl and Wilfrid Sellars, eds., *Readings in Philosophical Analysis*. New York: Appleton-Century-Crofts.

Rosten, Leo. 1968. *The Joys of Yiddish*. New York: McGraw-Hill.

Russell, Bertrand. 1956. On Denoting. In R. C. Marsh, ed., *Logic and Knowledge*. London: Allen and Unwin.

Russell, Bertrand. 1924. *Introduction to Mathematical Philosophy*. New York: Macmillan.

Russell, Bertrand and A. N. Whitehead. 1910. *Principia Mathematica*. Cambridge: Cambridge University Press.

Salmon, Wesley. 1977. A Third Dogma of Empiricism. In *Basic Problems in Methodology and Linguistics*. Dordrecht: Reidel.

Skyrms, Brian. 1966. *Choice and Chance*. Belmont, Calif.: Dickenson.

Smullyan, Raymond. 1980. *This Book Needs No Title*. Englewood Cliffs, N.J.: Prentice-Hall.

Turing, Alan M. 1950. Computing Machinery and Intelligence. *Mind* 59.

Watzlawick, Paul. 1977. *Behavior and Paradox*.

Wittgenstein, Ludwig. 1953. *The Philosophical Investigations*. Oxford: Blackwell.

Wittgenstein, Ludwig. 1961. *Tractatus Logico-Philosophicus*. Translated by D. F. Pears and B. F. McGuinness. London: Routledge and Kegan Paul.

INDEX